CITYSPOTS
BUDA

Carolyn Zukow

Written by Carolyn Zukowski
Updated by Sarah Cooper

Published by Thomas Cook Publishing
A division of Thomas Cook Tour Operations Limited
Company registration No: 1450464 England
The Thomas Cook Business Park, 9 Coningsby Road
Peterborough PE3 8SB, United Kingdom
Email: books@thomascook.com, Tel: +44 (0)1733 416477
www.thomascookpublishing.com

Produced by The Content Works Ltd
Aston Court, Kingsmead Business Park, Frederick Place
High Wycombe, Bucks HP11 1LA
www.thecontentworks.com

Series design based on an original concept by Studio 183 Limited

ISBN: 978-1-84157- 965-8

First edition © 2006 Thomas Cook Publishing
This second edition © 2008 Thomas Cook Publishing
Text © Thomas Cook Publishing
Maps © Thomas Cook Publishing/PCGraphics (UK) Limited
Transport map © Communicarta Limited

Series Editor: Kelly Anne Pipes
Production/DTP: Steven Collins

Printed and bound in Spain by GraphyCems

Cover photography (Castle Hill) © Panayiotou Paul/4Cornersimages.com

All rights reserved. No part of this publication may be reproduced, stored in a retrieval
system or transmitted, in any form or any means, electronic, mechanical, recording
or otherwise, in any part of the world, without prior permission of the publisher.
Requests for permission should be made to the publisher at the above address.

Although every care has been taken in compiling this publication, and the contents
are believed to be correct at the time of printing, Thomas Cook Tour Operations
Limited cannot accept any responsibility for errors or omission, however caused,
or for changes in details given in the guidebook, or for the consequences of any
reliance on the information provided. Descriptions and assessments are based on
the author's views and experiences when writing and do not necessarily represent
those of Thomas Cook Tour Operations Limited.

CONTENTS

CITYSPOTS

SYMBOLS KEY

The following symbols are used throughout this book:

ⓐ address ☎ telephone ⓕ fax ⓦ website address ⓔ email
🕒 opening times Ⓝ public transport connections ❶ important

The following symbols are used on the maps:

🛈 information office		points of interest	
✈ airport	O	city	
➕ hospital	O	large town	
🛡 police station	◦	small town	
🚍 bus station	=	motorway	
➁ railway station	—	main road	
Ⓜ metro	—	minor road	
✝ cathedral	—	railway	

❶ numbers denote featured cafés & restaurants

Hotels and restaurants are graded by approximate price as follows:
£ budget price ££ mid-range price £££ expensive

◗ *Budapest's extraordinary neo-Gothic Houses of Parliament*

INTRODUCING
Budapest

Introduction

While the rest of Hungary leisurely wakes up to the 21st century, Budapest has already had three coffee breaks and is zooming light years ahead. It's a city that's eager to adopt new trends while resolutely mindful of its dark and bullet-pocked past.

The key lies in understanding its history, marked by periods of great wealth and prosperity, and by devastating eras of political and social upheaval. Repeated warfare was inevitable due to the strategic location of Budapest, spreading out on either side of the Duna (River Danube) in the heart of Europe. The location of the city is strategic in a cultural sense as well. Baulking at the idea of being lumped with the Balkans or other Eastern European nations, Budapesters are proud that their 'Paris of the East' has inspired native sons Béla Bartók, László Bíró, Andy Grove and Ernő Rubik.

History braids itself with tradition while keeping its eye on the future. You will capture the digitalised, homely feeling of Budapest while sitting on a sleek, modernised tram as it zips quietly past weathered yet wonderfully regal architecture. Ten times larger than any other Hungarian city, this confident and cosmopolitan Magyar metropolis is a major European capital with heart. The neon lights and legions of tourists will only distract you briefly from its famous crooked, cobbled streets, secret alleyways, wide boulevards, atmospheric bridges and tranquil parks.

It's a city of largesse, with the best Turkish baths, the first metro system in continental Europe, the highest-ranked European 5-star hotel, the largest collection of Hungarian art anywhere, the second-largest synagogue in the world, the largest collection of preserved Soviet statuary outside Russia, the highest number of Jewish residents per capita of any European city and the most intact Jewish ghetto in Europe.

Mainly, it's a city of superlatives, doing its Buda*best* to keep you here longer than you intended.

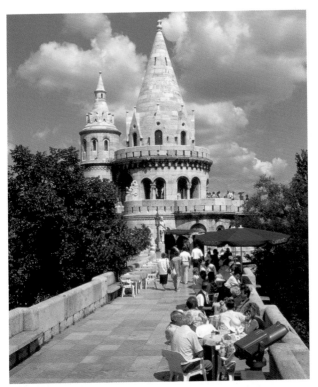

⬤ *Enjoy a drink on the terrace of the Fishermen's Bastion*

When to go

Budapest is a top destination at any time of year, though if you're sensitive to temperature, it's a good idea to avoid the extremes of summer and winter (see below). That aside, come whenever you like – there's no off-switch on Budapest's fun button!

SEASONS & CLIMATE

Budapest is fire and ice. Expect the summer to be very hot and dry, but with any luck a cool breeze will be blowing off the Danube. Autumn months are spectacular, but often chilly, and winter is downright cold, and sometimes snowy, with average temperatures between −4°C (25°F) and 4°C (39°F). Spring is the most pleasant time in the city, before the tourist season kicks off, though rain can dampen your spirits. Luckily, Budapest is a modern city offering comfortable public transport whatever the weather, and most places you will visit have air-conditioning and central heating.

ANNUAL EVENTS
March–April
Spring Festival The tourist season in Budapest kicks off with this month-long celebration, featuring world-class performers of classical music, opera, literature and theatre in a variety of glittery Budapest venues. There's also a series of open-air events, including parades and markets that beckon spring in with style. Ⓦ www.festivalcity.hu

Titanic International Film Festival (last week Mar–early Apr) Dozens of screenings of internationally acclaimed art and cult films from Asia, Europe and North America at venues across the city. Ⓦ www.titanicfilmfest.hu

Easter Monday (13 Apr 2009; 5 Apr 2010) This is largely an excuse to get drunk. In Budapest, men visit their girlfriends, spray them with cheap perfume and receive a stiff drink of *pálinka* (brandy) in return. The hangovers on Tuesday are brutal.

May

May Day (1 May) Once upon a time, this was a Communist holiday (Labour Day), but now it's just an excuse to go outside and listen to the open-air musical entertainment in the city's parks. Dance around the maypole, or go to a rock concert on the outdoor stage in Tabán in Buda.

⬥ The Budapest Wine Festival is an annual event held at the castle

June–August

Worldwide Music Day (closest weekend to Midsummer Day – 21 June)
This musical event is big throughout Hungary – every town features
some kind of concert. Budapest opens its doors (and ears) to jazz,
folk and rock musicians in the Városliget, Népliget and Klauzál parks.

Summer on the Chain Bridge (late June–mid-Aug) Every weekend
in early summer, the arts take over the Lánchíd (Chain Bridge),
which connects Buda and Pest, with a lively promenade of painters,
musicians, dancers and musical groups. Ⓦ www.festivalcity.hu

Budafest Summer Music Festival (July & Aug) A highbrow musical
event, where the venues are almost as stunning as the performances.
Ballet, folk, opera and jazz all feature. Ⓦ www.viparts.hu

Hungarian Formula One Grand Prix (Aug: see website for dates)
Book your tickets early for this event that brings the best and
brightest of Formula 1 racing into town. The course is about 20 km
(12 miles) from Budapest, in Mogyoród. Ⓦ www.formula1.com

Sziget Festival The city's magnificent music fest (see page 12).

St Stephen's Day (20 Aug) Hungarians celebrate their founding father
by taking his preserved right hand about town in a religious procession.
The climax features fireworks on top of Gellért Hill at 21.00.

Jewish Summer Festival (late Aug) A week-long celebration of Jewish
culture, featuring music, dance, comedy, cabaret and visual arts.
Ⓦ www.jewishfestival.hu

September–October

Budapest Wine Festival Every year, Budai Vár (Buda Castle) is the
venue for a highly competitive showdown of Hungarian wine
producers fiercely pitching their vintages. This is probably the
most fun you'll ever have at a trade fair. Ⓦ www.winefestival.hu

Budapest Autumn Festival The crème de la crème of Budapest's yearly events, a contemporary fine-arts festival featuring elements of dance, cinema and theatre. Ⓦ www.festivalcity.hu

Budapest International Marathon The city is transformed into a treadmill as thousands of runners descend to work up a sweat through the streets of both Buda and Pest. Ⓦ www.budapestmarathon.com

December

Karácsony (Christmas) From noon on 24 December until the evening of 26 December, the whole city shuts down to celebrate Christmas. Even if you're not into carp, the traditional Christmas meal eaten on Christmas Eve, try it just this once. Presents are exchanged on Christmas Eve, after dinner.

Szilveszterest (New Year's Eve) Fireworks blast all over town, and public transport runs all night to take you to the pre-, post- and post-post-midnight parties. The next day is an opportunity for re-affirming healthy resolutions.

PUBLIC HOLIDAYS
New Year's Day 1 Jan
Anniversary of the 1848–9 Uprising against the Habsburgs 15 Mar
Easter Monday 13 Apr 2009; 5 Apr 2010
May Day 1 May
St Stephen's Day 20 Aug
Anniversary of the 1956 Revolution, and of the 1989 Declaration of the Independent Republic of Hungary 23 Oct
Christmas Eve 24 Dec (half-day)
Christmas Day 25 Dec
Second Day of Christmas 26 Dec

The Sziget Festival

Every August, Óbudai Island in the middle of the Danube is the stage for a celebration of musical decadence: the Sziget (Island) Festival. Warm weather, cool vibes and some of the best musical acts combine to make this temporarily built festival city one of the hottest spots in Central Europe.

Some 1,000 different programmes at 60 different venues on the island attract more than 400,000 visitors during the seven days, offering not only music, but a wide range of sporting and cultural activities, theatre performances, fine-art exhibitions, literary readings and film screenings.

Alternative, blues, electric dance, hard-rock, hip-hop, mainstream, jazz and world music pours out of every corner of the island, creating a real buzz. But many of the most exquisite experiences have nothing to do with the music: drinking that first beer in the heat of the noonday sun, chilling out in chairs made of tyres while sipping an iced *macchiato*, setting up your tent in the early evening shadows and watching other music lovers in various states of bliss.

The festival organisers cater to your every need. There are accommodation and information offices; ATMs and bureaux de change; banking and postal services; children's activities and babysitting; restaurants, pubs, shops and craft markets; lockers and left-luggage facilities; a chemists; ground-keeping, hot showers and regularly pumped portable toilets – all take the rough out of roughing it. Police, firefighters and paramedics are on hand for emergencies. A multilingual information centre helps visitors to resolve any problems they might encounter during the week. You may even find yourself wandering into a 'Language First Aid' tent, where you can learn some basic Hungarian expressions to help you chat with the locals.

If you're not in the mood to groove, you can seek relief in bungee jumping, wall-climbing, football, volleyball and wide-open green spaces for tossing a frisbee.

There's a specially designed area on the island for caravans only. If you bring a car, you can park near the festival site or in a secure car park in Budapest. There are special buses, trains and ferries from Budapest to the festival grounds. The best bet, however, is to camp all week. You'll go home with a backpack full of smelly, beer-splashed, danced-out togs and a smile on your face. Go to Ⓦ www.sziget.hu for festival information.

🔺 *The Sziget Festival is the place to be in August*

History

For thousands of years, a blend of Celts, Romans, Huns, Mongols, Turks, Slovaks, Austrians, Germans and Russians have ransacked, razed and rebuilt Budapest many times over.

The Magyars, as Hungarians call themselves, were master equestrians from the steppes who rode and raided their way into Western Europe until halted by the Germanic tribes in 955. Their loss of power forced them into a reluctant alliance with the Holy Roman Empire, and, in the year 1000, the Magyar prince Stephen was crowned and the nation of Hungary was born. This didn't sit well with tribes loyal to the older shamanic religion, so they sent the missionary Gellért down a hill in a spiked barrel, hoping to get their message across.

Hungary was invaded by the Mongol hordes in the 13th century, and occupied by the Ottoman Turks in the 16th and 17th centuries. Buda developed into a provincial Ottoman town, Mátyás Templom (Matthias Church) was converted into a mosque and the hot springs underground were used to create Turkish baths.

In 1699 the Turks were ousted and the country became a province of the Austrian Habsburgs. Hungary blossomed economically and culturally, though a strong nationalistic undercurrent started to brew. Buda effectively became the German-speaking town of Ofen and by 1783 was the nation's administrative centre, while Pest became an important commercial centre. Soon, the nationalistic feelings came to the surface and Hungary declared independence in 1849. The Habsburgs were able to quell the uprising with the help of the Russian army.

Passive resistance among the Hungarians, and a couple of disastrous military defeats for the Habsburgs, eventually led to the Compromise of 1867, creating the Dual Monarchy of Austria the empire and Hungary the kingdom. As a result, Buda, Pest and Óbuda united to form Budapest in 1873. That same year, Jews were given equal rights in the courts and Budapest underwent a renaissance. A massive Jewish immigration movement brought scholars and industrialists from neighbouring Russia and Poland. Many of the buildings in Budapest that you see today were built during this exciting time.

The 20th century was a horror show, with Hungary on the losing side during both world wars. Budapest suffered severe damages in World War II, with the retreating German army blowing up Buda Castle and every bridge on the Danube. In 1949, the Communists gained control, banning books, executing foreign spies and imprisoning intelligentsia and church leaders. Again, an undercurrent of nationalism started to swell and resulted in an anti-Soviet uprising in Budapest, known as the 1956 revolution. The Russians retaliated, leaving thousands dead in the streets and many buildings scarred with bullet holes. The Russians knew that the Hungarians were hard to break, so they instituted a system of consumer-oriented communism, also known as 'goulash communism', transforming Hungary into the most liberal, furthest-developed and richest nation in the region until the 1980s. Following the collapse of communism, the nation became the Republic of Hungary in 1989.

In 2004, Hungary joined NATO and became a member of the EU. Budapest continues to be invaded, but this time by foreign investors hoping to make a killing in the property market. The riots of 2006, sparked by a leaked recording of the prime minister admitting to lying, were a blip on the country's upward trajectory and the city continues to be a Central European hotbed of development and enterprise.

Lifestyle

Budapest is built on a fault line, both physically and psychologically. Everywhere you go in the city you notice the new butting impatiently against the old. The younger generations fill the streets with new cars, mobile phones and a sense of purpose, while old people stare out of their windows lost in memories of shocking events that shook their lives. Façades of buildings carry scars of bullet holes made 50 years ago, while the house across the street has been renovated.

But if you think that shopping centres, hypermarkets and corporate logos will soon be taking over Budapest, think again. What makes Budapest so special is its ability to straddle this fault line, rebuilding history while allowing the tinge of the past to remain. This explains the lingering popularity of the Turkish baths, the handiworks sold by Transylvanian peasant women and the butcher who does a brisk business in the dingy blocks of flats on the city's outskirts. It also explains why Westernised holidays are lost on the modern Hungarian, who would rather stick with the traditional celebrations of name days than embrace the concept of Halloween or Valentine's Day.

The Hungarians are a proud people who have spent time convincing the world that they are not an Eastern European country, but a Central European country. To that end, the improvements made to infrastructure over the last five or ten years have not only improved the city, but also the people's outlook in general. International cuisine is now a mainstay of the capital along with service with a smile. The idea of good customer service is a notion that has stuck, and, with it, a new-found confidence in consumerism.

In the summer, Budapesters and their families all head to Lake Balaton (fondly referred to by landlocked locals as 'the Hungarian sea') for rest and relaxation, so don't expect to get any official business done on a Friday after 14.00. Hungarians are reasonable capitalists, meaning they will work hard for their money but never lose sight of the important things in life – family, friends and fun, and the freedom to choose when to take time off.

⬤ *Enjoying the sunshine in Heroes' Square*

Culture

As soon as you arrive in Budapest, pick up the latest issue of one of the English-language newspapers, the *Budapest Sun* or the *Budapest Times*. Sit down at a café, relax with a map and plot your adventure.

As you'll see, Budapest offers an exhausting list of cultural possibilities, and, what's more, almost every ticket is affordable. You can still go to the Állami Operaház (State Opera House, see page 81), one of Europe's finest, for less than five pounds, so it makes sense to go to a performance, even if you don't like opera or classical music. In the summer, churches and halls open their interiors to musical accompaniment and you'll hear exuberant strains of music along the Lánchíd (Chain Bridge) and in parks and gardens all over town.

The festivals in Budapest are the biggest cultural events of the year, showcasing the world's greatest musical, artistic and dramatic talents. The Sziget Festival (see page 12) is probably the best rock festival

BUDAPEST CARD

The *Budapest Kártya* (Budapest Card) provides unlimited travel on public transport, free entry to 60 museums and various sights, and discounts on everything from sightseeing tours to restaurant meals. Cards come in two- or three-day versions (6,450 HUF and 7,950 HUF respectively) and include a decent pocket-sized brochure containing maps of Buda, Pest and the metro system. The Budapest Card brochure map clearly indicates museums, galleries and other establishments that accept the card.

during the European summer, featuring an eclectic electric line-up of world-renowned rockers and their lesser-known counterparts.

Many performances at the modern **Nemzeti Színház** (**Hungarian National Theatre**, ❷ XI. Bajor Gizi Park 1 ❶ (1) 476 6800 Ⓦ www.nemzetiszinhaz.hu) are in English. Not only is it exciting to sit in the controversially designed theatre on the Pest embankment,

⬤ *The sumptuous interior of the State Opera House*

with a stage that can be raised or lowered, lifts that offer a panoramic view of the city and a façade that's half-submerged in a pool near the main entrance, but it is also a thrilling thespian adventure to hear Shakespeare with a Hungarian accent.

You can purchase tickets for events in a number of ways. For opera, ballet, theatre or concert tickets in advance, you can save money by going to the individual-venue box offices, as ticket agencies might not carry the entire price range of tickets. **Broadway Ticket Office** (ⓐ VI. Nagymező utca 19 ❶ (1) 302 3841) sells tickets to most cultural events. If you're trying to organise tickets from abroad, **Ticket Express** (ⓦ www.eventim.hu) is a good on-line bet. Ticket Express booking offices are also in convenient locations all over town.

Budapest's museums are unique in that they're high-class, without being snob fests. You'll find trendy galleries in the streets lined with public art. Some of the best museums in town, the Magyar Nemzeti Galéria (Hungarian National Gallery, see page 69) or the Szépművészeti Múzeum (Museum of Fine Arts, see page 94), not only house some incredible collections, but also boast buildings that are works of art in themselves. Go to ⓦ www.exindex.hu for details of temporary exhibitions in galleries around town.

The best source of listings for English-language films is the *Budapest Sun*. Movies labelled '*szinkronizált*', '*m.b.*' or '*magyarul beszélő*' are dubbed into Hungarian; those labelled '*feliratos*' have Hungarian subtitles.

End the evening with a stop at a café. As you come to the bitter end, you'll remember why you came here in the first place: not just for affordable fun and flash, but for a rich cultural experience.

🅞 *Night-time view across the Danube*

MAKING THE MOST OF
Budapest

Shopping

Budapest offers an incredibly diverse array of items and places in which to purchase them. You can layer your suitcases with flea-market finds, delectable deli foodstuffs, unique folk-inspired art and designer threads. It's refreshing to find the salespeople at global fashion giants twiddling their thumbs while the peasant women on the street corner do a brisk trade in embroidered one-of-a-kind handiworks.

Hungary is famous for its flashy equestrian gear, embroideries, painted eggs, folk costumes, hand-painted porcelain, crystal, Halas lace, decorative wood carvings and Helia-D cosmetics. Food items include red paprika, goose-liver pâté, pickled vegetables, Pick salami, or honey-soaked nuts in glass jars. If you're looking for a special

● *A shopping centre is dressed in its Christmas glory*

MARKETS

Budapest has some excellent *piac*, or markets, and they are
great places to get a food's-eye view of the locals. Vegetarians
will appreciate taking a break from the usual restaurant diet
of fried mushroom and cheese dishes to find the freshest
fruit, vegetables and bread. And, if you're after food on the
go, try an indoor fast-food stall. For a great introduction to the
region's foodstuffs, and to pack your picnic basket full, the best
place to go is the Nagyvásárcsarnok (Great Market Hall, see
page 98). This market is great for locally grown, fresh produce
and there are stalls selling salami, bread, fruit, nuts, poppy-
seed cakes and souvenirs. Or, try the **Bonbon Delicatesse**
(❷ V. Váci utca 11/b), one of the few places that serves
confectioneries, chocolates, spirits and wines, as well as
tasty pâté and other gourmet delights, after midnight.

The markets of Budapest also offer an overwhelming
assortment of antiques, folksy wares and contemporary
art. Falk Miksa utca, near Margit híd (Margaret Bridge), is a
thoroughfare featuring more than 20 shops with different
personalities in unusual settings.

The best shopping excitement is to be had at the flea
markets either in the Városliget (City Park) or at Ecseri (XIX.
Nagykőrösi út). These are strictly for the strong-willed shopper,
who can discern between treasure and trash. You'll benefit
from the Hungarian penchant for hoarding, be it coloured
bottles with glass stoppers, retro formica tables, light fittings,
weapons, medals, coins or Soviet and East German memorabilia.
Snap it up now before eBay gets a whiff of the action.

○ Rummage through the antique shops for special bargains

bottle, buy some Tokaji (sweet white) or Egri Bikavér (dry red) wines, *pálinka* (fiery fruit brandy) or the special hangover cure, Zwack Unicum.

Váci utca is the place to start. Little boutiques selling unique garments mingle with souvenir joints touting t-shirts, key rings and other forgettable items. There are also the more familiar outlets in the shape of **C&A** (② V. Váci utca 16 ❶ (1) 327 0024) and **Marks & Spencer** (② V. Váci utca 1–4 ❶ (1) 318 4606 or 267 0564). The fashion-conscious, or shoppers with children, will love the shopping complexes Westend City Center (see page 86), Mammut (see page 70) and **Mom Park** (② XII. Alkotás út 53 ❶ (1) 487 5501). Not places to save money, but these air-conditioned spaces are great for beating the summer heat.

Label-lovers will find garments galore on the prestigious Andrássy út, with its selection of exclusive shops. The Hungarian designer Katti Zoób (ⓦ www.kattizoob.hu) has her own outlet near Margit híd (Margaret Bridge), while around the Oktogon area are small retro shops selling funky designs from independent labels – Retrock is one of the best.

USEFUL SHOPPING PHRASES

How much is this?
Mennyibe kerül ez?
Mehnj-njee-beh keh-rewl ehz?

My size is ...
Az én méretem ...
Oz ehn may-reh-tehm ...

Can I try this on?
Felpróbálhatom?
Fehl-proh-bahl-ho-tom?

I'll take this one, thank you
Ezt megveszem, köszönöm
Ehzt mehg-veh-sehm, kuh-suh-nuhm

Eating & drinking

Influenced by neighbouring countries Austria, Croatia, Slovakia, Slovenia, Romania, Serbia and the Czech Republic, Hungary serves up hearty dishes rich in flavour and calories. A combination of French flair and wholesome goodness inspired by the hills and plains of Hungary makes a meal fit for a Magyar.

More and more restaurants in Budapest offer lighter fare, hoping to appeal to a more international palate. You'll find English-language menus in most Budapest restaurants, and friendly staff with some command of 'Hunglish', service-industry English. Modern restaurants aim to redesign the typically Hungarian dishes, offering pastas and big salads with some of the best home-grown produce in Europe. You will find that food isn't as cheap as you might expect, particularly in Pest, and if you order a bottle of imported wine with your meal, you could well run over budget.

Ever the traditionalists, Hungarians will reach for sauces rich in sour cream, fried goose liver and meat, including game such as boar and venison. Fish can feature on the Hungarian restaurant menu, especially carp or pike perch, often in the form of a thick spicy soup. Other traditional favourites include veal paprika stew, or roast chicken, with dumplings. Desserts, served with strong espresso, include strudels, *palacsinta* (sweet pancakes) and the legendary Gundel sponge cake

PRICE CATEGORIES

Restaurants with the following symbols indicate the cost of a three-course meal, excluding drinks.

£ up to 4,000 HUF   ££ 4,000–6,500 HUF   £££ over 6,500 HUF

soaked with rum and topped with chocolate sauce, walnuts, raisins and whipped cream.

Vegetarians will struggle here, as traditional Hungarian fare is meat-heavy. Fill up on the creamy mushroom or onion soups (often served in a hollowed-out bread loaf) or the cheese-stuffed, fried mushrooms.

Wine connoisseurs are familiar with the Hungarian sweet white wine, Tokaji, made by a special process where the grapes are left on the vine to sweeten and shrivel in the sun. Then it's rated by *puttony* number, or number of baskets of grapes that go into the barrel. The greater the number, the sweeter and more expensive the wine. Strong red Egri Bikavér (Bull's Blood) is internationally known and exported heavily in the EU. Hungary boasts 20 wine-producing districts that

⏹ *Al fresco dining in Franz Liszt Square*

make a wide range of wines, including Cabernet Sauvignon, Pinot Gris, Merlot, Riesling, Chardonnay, sparkling and rosé. It would be a shame not to try them all. One word of warning: it's considered bad taste to clink your beer or wine glasses. The occupying Austrians adopted this custom after they had executed the Hungarian generals who led the failed uprising of 1848–9.

End your meal with a warming shot of the 'digestive' Unicum. This secret blend of herbs and alcohol has been popular for generations and is considered a lifesaver by the locals. Its various uses are as a digestive, to get drunk on and to cure a killer hangover with come the morning. Makes sense.

When it is time to pay, you may notice a service charge tacked on to your bill. In this case, you don't have to tip unless your service was outstanding. If that's the case, then round up to the nearest hundred *forints*. If no service charge has been tacked on, add 10 per cent and round up to the nearest hundred *forints*.

Sweet cakes are a Turkish legacy and Budapest has many family-run *cukrászda* (cake shops) offering these Turkish-inspired delights in winding forgotten alleyways all over town. When it's warm, there are plenty of cheap little outdoor fast-food stalls in the Városliget (City Park) serving *lángos* (ring-shaped savoury doughnuts), pretzels and corn on the cob to stave off your hunger pangs.

Pastries and breads are a popular eat in Hungary. From the crescent-shaped buttery, biscuity *kifli* to the filling nut rolls, most delis and corner shops will have a range on offer. Perfect for breakfast or as a snack during the day, you can even find shops selling tiny versions of each pastry, allowing you to 'pick and mix' your cakes.

USEFUL DINING PHRASES

I would like a table for ... people
Szeretnék egy asztalt ... személyre
Seh-reht-nayk ehdj os-tolt ... seh-mayy-reh

May I have the bill, please?
Kérhetem a számlát?
Kayr-heh-tehm o sahm-laht?

Waiter/Waitress!
Pincér/Pincérnő!
Pin-cayr/pin-cayr-nur!

Could I have it well-cooked/medium rare, please?
Kaphatnám ezt jól megsülten/félig sülten?
Kop-hot-nahm ehzt johl mehg-shewl-tehn/
fay-leeg shewl-tehn?

I am a vegetarian. Does this contain meat?
Vegetáriánus vagyok. Van ebben hús?
Veh-geh-tah-ree-ah-nosh vodjok. Von ehb-behn hoosh?

Where is the toilet (restroom) please?
Hol van a WC?
Hohl von o vay-tsay?

I would like a cup of/two cups of/another coffee/tea
Szeretnék egy csésze/két csésze kávét/még egy kávét/teát
Seh-reht-nayk ehdj chay-seh/kayt chay-she kah-veht/mayg
ehdj kah-veht/teh-aht

Entertainment & nightlife

Budapest is open non-stop for a good time and offers something for everyone, from calm cafés to brash and bawdy transvestite shows. Most of the action happens in Pest: Liszt Ferenc tér and Ráday utca brim with fashionable venues and restaurants.

Be prepared to walk between venues, where you'll find jazz, blues, rock, disco, gypsy, Balkan and Hungarian folk music, all elbowing for your attention at the smoky, raucous clubs and bars. Most bars are open until 02.00; clubs continue until 04.00, though some stay open until dawn.

Budapest has a great club scene, featuring everything from hip-hop to salsa grooves, and the cover charges are very reasonable. One of the most unique venues can be found at the Király Fürdő (King's Baths, see page 69). On regularly scheduled evenings, they turn into a steamy, trip-hop splash pad, with light reflecting off the steam as you groove in the water.

The *borozó* (wine cellar) is a Budapest institution. These smoky cavernous rooms are usually filled with older men drinking cheap, but decent, wine and arguing over politics. Women, especially single women, will not feel welcome. The *söröző* (beer house) is more of a social place, where you can find good, affordable food and a more mixed group of locals, expats and foreign travellers.

If gambling's your thing, Budapest has over a dozen casinos, most of which are in the luxury hotels along the Duna korzó. Formal dress and a big wad of cash is often a prerequisite for entry, though many now accept credit cards.

The Petőfi Csarnok (ⓐ XIV. Zichy Mihály út 14 ⓘ (01) 363 3730 ⓦ www.petoficsarnok.hu), in the Városliget, and the **Almássy téri Szabadidő Központ** (ⓐ VII. Almássy tér 6) are the two favourite venues for small pop concerts and folk music. International stars perform at the Puskás Ferenc Stadion, the main sports stadium, also known as Népstadion (see page 32). Purchase tickets for rock and jazz at **TEX Ticket Express** in Déli pályaudvar metro (🚇 VI. Andrássy út 18) and **Publika** (🚇 VII. Károly körút 9).

The on-line resource 🌐 www.caboodle.hu is probably the best source of nightlife listings in Budapest. English-speaking revellers will also want to pick up a copy of *Budapest Week* (🌐 www.budapestweek.com), *Budapest Funzine* (🌐 www.funzine.hu) or the *Budapest Sun* (🌐 www.budapestsun.com). *Where Budapest* is a useful monthly guide in English, available free at most hotels.

🔺 *Fireworks over the Danube*

Sport & relaxation

SPECTATOR SPORTS

Hungary's long and illustrious sporting tradition has sprouted more Olympic gold medallists per capita than any other country in the world. You may notice early in the mornings (on your way back from a night of clubbing) the throngs of schoolchildren who are forced into the water or on to the training field.

Although Hungarians are great individual athletes, they've had a hard time making it big in the sporting world. Apathetic fans, corruption, underfunding of sports teams and political problems have all contributed to the fact that Hungary's sporting teams haven't qualified for any major league championship since 1986. The football team **Ferencváros** (🐾 www.ftc.hu) is the most successful club.

The best venue to view sporting events is the massive, Soviet-inspired **Puskás Ferenc Stadion** (🅰 XIV. Istvánmezei út 1–3 🚇 Metro: Stadionok).

PARTICIPATION SPORTS

Budapest is a big city and, even with a great metro system, you'll find your fitness level improved just by walking. Luckily, Budapest has some excellent parks and ambling spots. From Gellért Hill, you'll be treated to spectacular views of the city below, and as you walk along the Széchenyi rakpart leading to Margitsziget (Margaret Island, see page 109), you'll find boats moored on the quays with lots of cafés on board. Margaret Island is Budapest's playground that will exhaust you with opportunities to ride in a pedal car, toss a Frisbee or jog on the cushioned path snaking round the island, while the Városliget (City Park, see page 93) is a great place to meander along the lake and go boating in summer or skating in winter.

Budapest Madness (www.budapestmadness.com) is a tour agency that specialises in hedonistic English-speaking group tours at very reasonable prices. They organise a heap of fun programmes that include Trabant (a funny little East German car that was popular during the Communist regime) rallies, thermal-bath crawls and helicopter tours over the city.

RELAXATION

The most tranquil way to relax in Budapest is to head to one of the city's baths. Try the Gellért Fürdő (Gellért Baths, see page 67) or the Széchenyi Baths (see page 46), not only to soak tired muscles, but also to lift your spirits after a long night out on the town.

● *Locals ice skating next to Buda Castle*

Accommodation

Budapest boasts some excellent accommodation options for the visitor. Whether you're into luxurious hotels offering bathing cures, chic self-catering apartments, funky budget digs or campsites, Budapest has it all.

Central Pest is where you'll find some of the nicest hotels, but they do come at a premium. If money is tight, try the outskirts of town. Good public transport allows easy access to the city centre.

The boom of renovation has had a definite effect on the quality of rooms. Many 3-star hotels are well designed and provide amenities such as international TV stations, internet access, lifts, laundry and air-conditioning. All hotels in Hungary are obliged to have a certain number of non-smoking rooms.

Hungarian *panzió* (bed and breakfasts) are family-run places with a personal touch. However, that personal touch may scream 'kitsch disaster', so ask to see a room before you commit.

Renting a self-catering apartment in the centre of town is a great way to save money and feel local. Use a reputable agency, such as IBUSZ (see page 119) or **OHB** (Ⓦ www.ohb.hu). Good deals can sometimes be made with an old lady tout at the railway station, but ask to see a map to check the location before you go traipsing off into the sunset.

PRICE CATEGORIES

This selection of accommodation is rated by price for a double room including breakfast.

£ up to 15,000 HUF   ££ 15,000–25,000 HUF   £££ over 25,000 HUF

Camping is excellent in Buda – the grass is definitely greener a short distance from the hectic pace of town. Don't pitch your tent illegally in any of Budapest's green areas, or you will be fined.

You can find more information about accommodation on-line at Ⓦ www.hotelinfo.hu, Ⓦ www.hotels.hu or the **Hungarian National Tourist Board** site (Ⓦ www.hungarytourism.hu). Once you're in town, your best bet is to go to one of the Tourinform offices (see page 153). IBUSZ is happy to book you into any hotel, apartment or hostel, and they don't charge a booking fee.

HOTELS

Amigo Hostel £ What this place lacks in space it makes up for in friendliness, location and value. ⓐ VI. Liszt Ferenc tér 4 ❶ (1) 332 6322 Ⓦ www.amigohostel.hu

Connection Gay Guest House £ A friendly, welcoming environment for gays, lesbians and straights. Bright, clean rooms with a view on to a courtyard and gracious amenities. ⓐ VII. Király utca 41 ❶ (1) 267 7104 ⓔ guesthouse@connection.hu

easyHotel Budapest Oktogon £ Basic but in a prime position and good value for money. ⓐ VI. Eötvös utca 25/a ❶ On-line booking only at Ⓦ www.easyhotel.com

Baross Hotel ££ A peaceful hotel, many of whose light and airy rooms face onto a courtyard. ⓐ VII. Baross utca 15 ❶ (1) 461 3010 Ⓦ www.barosshotel.hu ⓔ info@barosshotel.hu

Boat Hotel Fortuna ££ A converted river cruiser turned mini luxury liner, with wood panelling, brass fittings and chandeliers. Cheaper hostel accommodation with shared bathroom facilities in the hull, so you can get that touch of class for less. ❸ XIII. Szent István körút, Budai Alsó rakpart ❶ (1) 288 8100 ❾ www.fortunahajo.hu ❺ fortunahajo@chello.hu

City Hotel Pilvax ££ This quality hotel features clean, air-conditioned rooms. ❸ V. Pilvax köz 1–3 ❶ (1) 266 7660 ❾ www.cityhotels.hu ❺ sales@cityhotels.hu

Hotel Benczúr ££ A large hotel with modern rooms and a minimalist 1970s approach in many of the common areas. ❸ VI. Benczúr utca 35 ❶ (1) 479 5650 ❾ www.hotelbenczur.hu ❺ info@hotelbenczur.hu

Kulturinnov ££ A smallish hotel on a picture-perfect street in a sought-after location. ❸ I. Szentháromság tér 6 ❶ (1) 224 8102 or 224 4105 ❺ mka@mail.datanet.hu

Leó Panzió ££ Lots of cherry-wood furniture and royal colours combine to make this a stay fit for a king. Perfectly located, with spacious rooms and high ceilings. ❸ V. Kossuth Lajos utca 2/a ❶ (1) 266 9041 ❾ www.leopanzio.hu ❺ leo@leopanzio.hu

Atrium £££ A contemporary and sleek hotel with sound-proofed windows. ❸ VII. Csokonai utca 14 ❶ (1) 299 0777 ❾ www.atriumhotelbudapest.com ❺ sales@atriumhotelbudapest.com

Danubius Hotel Gellért £££ Ornate historical interiors with views over the Danube. What's more, guests have access to the celebrated Gellért Baths (see page 67). ❸ XI. Szent Gellért tér 1 ❶ (1) 889 5500 ❾ www.danubiushotels.com/gellert ❺ gellert.reservation@danubiusgroup.com

⬥ *The City Hotel Pilvax enjoys a central but quiet location*

Lánchíd 19 £££ A very plush modern hotel, affording some of the best views seen from a bath tub in the city. ⊖ I. Lánchíd utca 19 ⬥ 06 800 122 36 (toll free) ⓦ www.designhotels.com/lanchid ⓔ res@designhotels.com

○ *Top-of-the-range accommodation at Danubius Hotel Gellért*

Mercure Korona £££ Well-located, large hotel with excellent facilities and a mellow, street-level lounge. Take a dip in the pool to cool off. ⓐ V. Kecskeméti utca 14 ❶ (1) 486 8800 ⓦ www.mercure-korona.hu ⓔ h1765@accorhotels.com

New York Palace £££ A luxurious hotel occupying an opulent building. It even has a basement spa designed to represent an ice cave, perfect as a respite from the Hungarian summer heat. ⓐ VI. Erzsébet körút 9–11 ❶ (1) 886 6111 ⓦ www.newyorkpalace.hu ⓔ info@newyorkpalace.hu

HOSTELS

Art Guest House £ With a refreshing absence of bunk beds, this non-smoking hostel is only a short walk from Nyugati railway station, with no curfews or lockouts, a clean kitchen and a free internet

terminal. ⓐ V. Podmaniczky utca 19 (doorbell ART) ① (1) 302 3739
ⓔ artguests@citromail.hu

Citadella Hotel and Hostel £ Great views as it sits atop Gellért Hill in
an historic fortress with atmosphere to spare. ⓐ XI. Citadella sétány
① (1) 466 5794 Ⓦ www.citadella.hu ⓔ hotel@citadella.hu

Hostel Marco Polo £ Probably the cleanest and friendliest hostel in town.
Doubles, quads and roomy dorms on offer with a pleasant courtyard,
cheap internet facilities and a bar. ⓐ VII. Nyár utca 6 ① (1) 413 2555
Ⓦ www.marcopolohostel.com ⓔ sales@marcopolohostel.com

Mellow Mood Central Hostel £ Offering a range of air-conditioned
rooms, from en suite twins to eight-bed dorms, this clean hostel is
popular with backpackers and located a short walk from Váci utca.
ⓐ V. Bécsi utca 2 ① (1) 411 1310 ⓔ info@mellowmoodhostel.com

Red Bus Hostel £ A centrally located, reasonably priced hostel, with
its own second-hand English bookshop. ⓐ V. Semmelweis utca 14
① (1) 266 0136 Ⓦ www.redbusbudapest.hu

CAMPSITES

Plan on spending about 2,500 HUF to pitch your tent and 3,500 HUF to
park your caravan. There are several campsites in Budapest, but for the
location and amenities (such as laundry facilities and pool), and friendly
service, **Római Kemping** (ⓐ III. Szentendrei út 189 ① (1) 388 7176
ⓔ romai@message.hu) is the best place to rest. Other popular campsites
include **Orion Camping Budapest** (ⓐ XIII. Népsziget, Népsziget út – Zsilip
utca ⓔ info@budapestcamping.hu) and **Zugligeti Niche Camping**
(ⓐ XII. Zugligeti út 101 ① (1) 200 8346 Ⓦ www.campingniche.hu).

THE BEST OF BUDAPEST

Whether you're on a flying visit to Budapest, or taking a more leisurely break in Hungary, the city offers sights and experiences that should not be missed.

TOP 10 ATTRACTIONS

- **Országház (Houses of Parliament)** Laid languidly along the banks of the Danube, the city's political powerhouse seems to possess a spire for every day of the year (see page 78)

- **Houses of Worship** Szent István Bazilika (St Stephen's Basilica), Mátyás Templom (Matthias Church) and Nagy Zsinagóga (Great Synagogue) – superlative-filled houses of God reflect the diverse paths of religion in Budapest (see pages 84, 66 and 96)

- **Budavári Sikló (Buda Castle Funicular)** Lends new meaning to the phrase 'hanging out' (see page 62)

- **Halászbástya (Fishermen's Bastion)** The bird's-eye view over Pest is stunning, and so is the neo-Romanesque structure that you mount to enjoy it (see page 65)

- **Váci utca** The buzzing heart of Budapest positively throbs with atmospheric pubs, charismatic bars and beautiful boutiques; every visitor should get with the Váci vibe at some point in their trip (see pages 90 & 100)

- **Gellért Fürdő (Gellért Baths)** Relaxing muscles that you didn't even know were tense while soaking up the traditional – nay, decadent – ambience of this art nouveau lounge-arama really is the only sensible way of purging yourself of that last scintilla of stress (see page 67)

- **Margitsziget (Margaret Island)** This smack-in-the-middle-of-the-Danube outpost of paradise contains what must be Budapest's zenith of kitsch – a fountain that erupts to the sound of (badly) recorded muzak (see page 109)

- **Magyar Nemzeti Galéria (Hungarian National Gallery)** The most valuable collection of Hungarian art in the world (see page 69)

- **Állami Operaház (State Opera House)** Built to rival all great opera houses in its opulence, but actually offering affordable tickets, this hints at what the Communist experiment could have been like (see page 81)

- **Szoborpark (Statue Park)** Ha! Who needs loveable mice when you can fill an entire theme park with reminders of those crazy days of Communist public art? Well, it's an angle... (see page 110)

⬤ *Get a great view of the Houses of Parliament from the river*

Suggested itineraries

HALF-DAY: BUDAPEST IN A HURRY

Take the funicular up to the carefree and car-free Castle district, a UNESCO World Heritage Site. If it's raining, take an hour to look at the world-renowned masterpieces at the Hungarian National Gallery (see page 69). From there, it's on to Buda Castle (see page 62) and the neo-Gothic Matthias Church (see page 66). Then, make your way to the sun-bleached Halászbástya (Fishermen's Bastion, see page 65) and climb the turrets, which afford possibly the finest views of Pest from across the Danube.

1 DAY: TIME TO SEE A LITTLE MORE

If you have a full day, walk along the embankment, admiring the boat traffic moving along the Danube as you cross Margit híd (Margaret Bridge). Pick up tram 2 at Jászai Mari tér, which will take you on a riverside circuit, passing some of the most important buildings of town. You'll take in the Országház (Houses of Parliament, see page 78), grand hotels such as Gresham Palace (see page 82) and, finally, the **Corvinus University of Budapest** (🌐 www.uni-corvinus.hu). From there, you get a beautiful view of Gellért Hill across the Danube. Cross the Szabadság híd (Liberty Bridge) and end your day by visiting the Danubius Hotel Gellért (see page 36), which has one of the most luxurious thermal baths in Budapest. Walk back over the bridge and spend the evening window shopping along Váci utca, Budapest's main shopping district and pedestrianised thoroughfare.

2–3 DAYS: TIME TO SEE MUCH MORE

To get a closer look at Budapest, you can see all the above sights, plus take in some other areas of interest. If the weather's nice, or you have

● A view of Margaret Bridge from the Tabán

children, go to the Városliget (City Park, see page 93), which has some grandiose spaces to explore, including the Museum of Fine Arts (see page 94) and Hősök tere (Heroes' Square, see page 93), or to Margaret Island, a tranquil oasis in the middle of the Danube.

LONGER: ENJOYING BUDAPEST TO THE FULL

With four or more days, you can see all the above sights, as well as climb Gellért Hill, stop off at the Sziklatemplom (Cave Church, see page 66) and go on to the Citadel (see page 65). With a bit more time, you'll be able to catch an opera performance in the evening or take a day trip to Hungary's favourite little town, Szentendre (see page 114).

Something for nothing

In Budapest, fun is fundamentally free. Catching trams 4 or 6 on Margaret Bridge will take you on a semi-circle circuit through the main areas of Pest, including Oktogon and Blaha Lujza tér; hopping onto tram 2 at Jászai Mari tér will take you on a grand tour of Budapest's main sights along the Danube for the price of a tram ticket. From there, try a little window shopping along Váci utca, Budapest's pedestrian-friendly life vein. As you walk along, you can admire the buskers and street performers for, well, free.

Budapest is brimming with museums, with admission for adults ranging from only 800–1,200 HUF and some even offering free admission to permanent exhibitions. The most impressive include the free-entry **Magyar Nemzeti Múzeum (Hungarian National Museum ❸** VIII. Múzeum körút 14–16 ❶ (1) 338 2122), the Hungarian National Gallery (see page 69) and the Museum of Fine Arts (see page 94). Budapest's most beautiful churches are free to visit, including Szent István Bazilika (St Stephen's Basilica, see page 84), and you can even get a close look at the macabre sight of St Stephen's shrivelled-up forearm, displayed in a small glass cabinet. Other free entries include Cave Church (see page 66), hewn into the side of Gellért Hill by Pauline monks, and the Inner City Parish Church (see page 92), the oldest building in Pest.

For a unique insight into Hungarian history, visit **Kerepesi Cemetery** (❸ VIII Kerepesi temetö), close to Keleti train station. This is the final resting place of the famous and the revered; the cemetery is filled with elaborate statues, striking frescoes and massive mausoleums. It's a sober opportunity for historical, artistic and personal reflection.

Margaret Island (see page 109) is Budapest's playground, smack in the middle of the Danube. This 2.5 km (one-and-a-half miles) of gentle

🔺 *The Hungarian National Museum is just one of the many free museums*

parks and leafy picnic spots is part of the green belt of Budapest. Here you can wander the tree-lined paths, passing thermal spas, landmark monuments and ancient ruins. It's free to stick your toes in the water, but watch out for turtles, and there's also the dramatic water fountain that erupts sporadically into life against a backdrop of recorded classical music.

Entrance to Budapest's baths can cost anything up to 3,100 HUF. However, in many baths (including both the Gellért and Széchenyi baths), you receive money back if you leave before your time is up. So if you pay, say, 2,300 HUF to get into the Széchenyi Baths, and you leave within two hours, you will receive money back on the way out, depending on how long you've stayed.

When it rains

When it's raining cats and dogs, you have to think like a fish. The best way to beat the weather blues is to partake in one of Budapest's finest traditions ... the bath. Make your way to the **Széchenyi Baths** (❸ XIV. Állatkerti körút 11 ❶ (1) 363 3210) in the Városliget (City Park). This old complex of indoor and outdoor pools is the deepest, hottest and largest bathing facility in Budapest. After a good soak, you'll be ready to visit one of the beer houses nearby. One of the best beer houses in Budapest is **Bajor Sörsátor** (❷ Kós Károly sétány), where beer-drinking is considered a spectator sport, and wine is quaffed straight out of the barrel.

While you are near the Városliget, why not try the Állatkert, or zoo (see page 148)? It may seem like a strange choice, but at least you won't have to worry about crowds, and there are plenty of exhibits inside. An exotic bird house, palm house, aquarium and indoor play area for children make this one of the best places to while away the bad weather.

If zoos aren't your thing, you could try a museum or two. Not far from the Városliget, you'll find two interesting museums to escape the dreary weather. The Museum of Fine Arts (see page 94) houses the largest collection of international art in Hungary. Rumour has it that there are more El Grecos here than in Spain. The House of Terror Museum (see page 98) is definitely the kind of place you want to visit on a dreary day. This award-winning controversial exhibition memorialises the cruelties committed during the German and Soviet occupations of Hungary.

When the heavens open, it's time to head underground. Pálvölgyi Stalactite Cave (see page 110) is resplendent in fossils, aragonite crystals and coffee-coloured stalactites. The thermal waters channelled through the stone also create gorgeous graduations of colour in the walls. Tours take place regularly throughout the day and a guide reveals how once upon a time, Hungary was underwater. Ancient history and geography have never been so interesting.

Cinemas and indoor shopping centres also provide a welcome respite. The Westend City Center (see page 86) has more than 400 shops and services to keep you busy on a rainy day. The multiplex cinema shows new releases of English-language films.

So, you see, a rainy day doesn't have to make you feel like a fish out of water. You just have to go with the flow.

🔺 *Get wet indoors at the Gellért Baths (see page 67)*

On arrival

TIME DIFFERENCE
Hungary follows Central European Time, which is one hour ahead of GMT.

ARRIVING
By air
Getting into Budapest from the airport, **Budapest Ferihegy Airport**
(❸ 1675 Budapest Ferihegy ❶ (1) 296 9696 ❿ www.bud.hu) is a piece
of cake. The easiest way to get into town is by the **Airport Minibus**
(❶ (1) 296 8555). As you exit the arrivals hall, go up to the counter, give
them your name and desired location, and they will pack you on your
way in air-conditioned comfort. Save more money by booking a return
ticket (single 2,490 HUF, return 4,390 HUF; two persons 4,490 HUF).
On your return, book the Airport Minibus 24 hours in advance.

   A taxi from the airport costs only a tad more. Some taxis offer
fixed prices from the airport to town. **Tele5Taxi** (❶ (1) 555 5555)
charges 4,600 HUF to Pest and 5,100 to Buda. If they're not standing
outside the airport, ask someone at the information desk to call for
you, or try **City Taxi** (❶ (1) 211 1111) or **Fő Taxi** (❶ (1) 222 2222), who
have similar fixed rates.

   The bus from the airport is by far the cheapest option, but will
require you to become familiar with the public transport system
first. When exiting the airport, find the bus stop that says 'BKV Plusz
Reptér busz'. The bus stops at the airport every 15 minutes, from 04.55
to 23.20. It goes to Kőbánya-Kispest metro station (on the blue line),
20 minutes away. From there, take the metro into town. This takes
20 to 25 minutes to reach Deák Ferenc tér in central Pest. Purchase
bus tickets from the orange vending machines outside Terminal 2A
or next to the stop, or from the newspaper kiosk inside Terminal 2B.

By rail

Budapest has three major railway stations: **Déli pályaudvar** – the southern railway station – (ⓐ I. Krisztina körút 37 ❶ (1) 375 6593); **Keleti pályaudvar** – the eastern railway station – (ⓐ VIII. Rákóczi út ❶ (1) 413 4610); and **Nyugati pályaudvar** – the western railway station – (ⓐ VI. Nyugati tér ❶ (1) 349 8503). Each is conveniently connected to the metro system as well as to other public transport. All have bureaux de change, left-luggage facilities, public phones and information desks. For any information about the stations or timetable, call ❶ 06 40 494 949 for English and Hungarian speakers, or, from abroad, call ❶ +36 1 371 9449.

⬤ Budapest has the oldest metro system in continental Europe

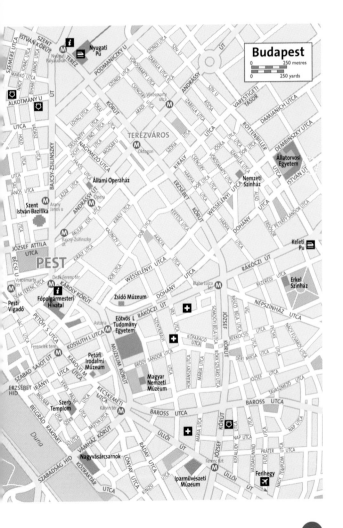

Budapest

0 ——— 250 metres
0 ——— 250 yards

By road

The M1, M3, M5 and M7 are toll motorways that will link you to Budapest from all directions. Driving in Budapest isn't recommended, as many of the thoroughfares near the sights and tourist areas are pedestrian-only. Park your car in one of the many centrally located multi-storey car parks, and you'll be well on your way.

If you get into car trouble, the **Hungarian Automobile Club** (🕿 (1) 345 1800) offers 24-hour roadside assistance and emergency roadside help (🕿 188).

FINDING YOUR FEET

Let's face it – Budapest is big. But it's beautiful in the way that it routes heavy traffic around the centre, making many of the centrally located tourist sections an ambler's heaven. It's also heaven for

🔽 *Use the Danube to find your bearings*

pickpockets, so keep your valuables at your side and don't let yourself get too distracted by the beautiful scenery. The cobbled streets can play havoc with heels so wear comfortable shoes.

ORIENTATION

The Duna (Danube) runs north–south through Budapest, separating the city into Buda (to the west) and Pest (to the east). For bucolic beauty, quiet streets and great views, head for the hills – the Buda Hills, that is. For the glitz and glamour of city life, go to Pest. Some of the most striking architecture in Budapest is along the Danube, which is perfect for strolling.

The best way to get your bearings is to walk along the Danube embankment, on the Pest side, from Március 15 tér to Roosevelt tér. Outdoor cafés and benches sprawl out next to hotel fronts with great views of Castle Hill, looming over the other side of the Danube. Sitting on the railings along the tram line at Vigadó tér is the statue of the

MAKING SENSE OF BUDAPEST ADDRESSES

Addresses in Budapest are as clear as, well, Hungarian, but there's a method to what seems to be madness. Budapest addresses begin with the number of the district. There are 23 districts in Budapest, labelled in Roman numerals, the most central being the I., V. and VII. (first, fifth and seventh) districts. Take, for example, V. Petőfi tér. Petőfi tér is the street name, and it's in the V. district, so you know it's central. '*Tér*' means 'square', while '*utca*' means 'street' and '*út*' means 'road' so be clear as to whether you're heading for a street or a road – there is the tourist strip of Váci utca but also a pretty dull Váci út, both of which are in Pest.

In a typical Budapest home address, a combination of three numerals then follows the street name, for example, Kossuth Lajos utca 14. III. 24. The first numeral after the street name denotes the number of the apartment building, the second numeral the number of the floor and the third numeral the number of the individual apartment. Confusingly, some old buildings in Pest are designated as having a half-floor, or upper-ground floor, between the ground and first floor proper – so what the British would call the second floor, and Americans the third, Hungarians might describe as the first.

'Little Princess'. From there, make your way to Váci utca. This chic pedestrianised street is the heart of Budapest, perfect for window-shopping and people-watching. Here you can buy a large map of the town, sit down at one of the many comfortable cafés and plan your visit. Otherwise, take tram 4 or 6 from Margaret Bridge, which will take you on a very cheap, semi-circle tour of Pest.

GETTING AROUND

Public transport has a long history in Budapest; it has the oldest metro system in continental Europe. Luckily, all of Budapest's treasures are easily accessible on foot or by the **Budapest Public Transport Company** (BKV, Ⓦ www.bkv.hu). The BKV operates metro lines (M1, yellow; M2, red; M3, blue), blue local buses, yellow trams and red trolleybuses, which generally run from 04.30 to 23.00. Prior to boarding purchase your tickets at metro stations, newsagents or hotels. You must validate your tickets in a ticket puncher and present them, upon request, to an inspector. It makes no sense to ride without a valid ticket; inspectors check tickets frequently on all lines, stepping onto the bus or tram wearing casual clothes and then putting on their official armband and badges. If you buy the Budapest Card (see page 18), then your travel on all public transport is covered; if you're not interested in the Budapest Card, then it's more economical to buy one of the one-, three- or seven-day metro passes (from 1,550 HUF) or a book of ten tickets (2,350 HUF), so that you're not constantly fishing around for change.

IF YOU GET LOST, TRY ...

Excuse me, do you speak English?
Elnézést, beszél angolul?
Ehl-nay-zaysht, beh-sayl on-goh-lool?

Can you point to it on my map?
Meg tudná ezt mutatni a térképemen?
Mehg tood-nah ehzt moo-tot-nee o tayr-kay-peh-mehn?

If you're over 65 and an EU citizen, you can ride the HÉV trains for free. You will need to show proof of identification, so if you look fifty-something rather than sixty-something, it's best to keep your passport to hand. Similarly, all EU citizens under the age of 26 can get discounted train travel on weekends.

Taking a taxi is simple. By law, taxis cannot charge more than the following amounts anywhere in Budapest: from 06.00–22.00, a 300-HUF basic fee, then 240 HUF for each additional one km (half-mile) or 60 HUF a minute. Waiting costs 70 HUF per minute. From 22.00–06.00, the price increases to a 420 HUF basic fee, then 336 HUF for each additional one km (half-mile), or 84 HUF a minute.

All taxis must have working meters and be able to issue a receipt. City Taxi and Fő Taxi (see page 48) have a trustworthy reputation. Taxi drivers will expect a small tip at the end of the journey. Add 10 per cent and round up to the nearest hundred *forints*.

CAR HIRE

Hiring a car in Budapest makes no sense, unless you're planning to take a trip out into the country. For the best discounts (up to 50 per cent, in some cases), you need to book ahead and on-line. The following companies have offices in the airport and in town, and are generally open from Monday to Friday, from 08.00 to 20.00.

Budget Rent a Car ❶ (1) 214 0420 Ⓦ www.budget.hu

Europcar Inc ❶ (1) 296 8105 Ⓦ www.europcar.com

FOX Autorent Owned and run by Hungarians; cheaper than the big guys ❶ (1) 382 9000 Ⓦ www.fox-autorent.com

Hertz ❶ (1) 296 7171 Ⓦ www.hertz.com

Kemwel ❶ (1) 214 0420 Ⓦ www.kemwel.com

▶ *The Chain Bridge elegantly spans the Danube*

Buda: the Castle District, Gellért Hill & Tabán

These three small districts in Buda contain a textbook's worth of historical sights and are a stronghold of the Hungarian psyche: strong enough to look back into the treachery of the past, smart enough to continue forward. This area of town is now home to some of Budapest's most sought-after addresses and swankiest restaurants.

A UNESCO World Heritage Site, Buda is the *grande dame* of Budapest, surviving at all costs. Its streets are filled with ivy-clad history, vista-rich villas, Gothic arches, and hired horsemen with carriages and tourists, lots of them. It's no wonder; you really can't visit Budapest without spending time in the Castle District, to see where it all began. Buda is an ancient Slavic word meaning 'hut' or 'small dwelling', and that's what originally stood in this area until the advancement of the Mongol hordes in the 13th century. King Béla built the first fortress here, a stronghold that has been rebuilt several times throughout history with the invasions of Turks and Habsburgs. It still bears the bullet scars of the last conflict in 1945 as the Germans retreated.

When the Pope sent Bishop Gellért to oversee the coronation of King Stephen (later, St Stephen), and to convert the wayward Magyars, he was greeted very differently than he expected. The ungrateful masses tossed Bishop Gellért down the hill in a spiked barrel. At the top of Gellért Hill, the Felszabadulási Emlékmű (Liberation Monument) stands (see page 65), created to honour Soviet soldiers who 'liberated' Hungary from the Germans. Even further uphill, the Citadel sits (see page 64), built by the Habsburgs to keep a watchful eye and maintain an intimidating presence over the city. The views from here are among the best in the city; join tourists and locals alike on the well-maintained walking paths.

Tabán's terraced gardens of today hide the footsteps of Buda's founding fathers. On the site where Buda's first Celts settled, Romans dominated and Turks bathed, and where a slum inhabited by Serbs, Greeks and Gypsies once stood, Tabán is now a summer outdoor music venue.

The best way to approach this area of town is to take the Buda Castle Funicular from Clark Ádám tér. If you're more likely to feel vertiginous than thrilled by the view from the funicular, you can climb up the twisting walkway that leads from Clark Ádám tér, or even take the lift that leaves from Dózsa György tér. The Várbusz (Castle Bus) also runs from Moszkva tér. Once you've made it to the top, plan on a lot of easy ambling between sights.

SIGHTS & ATTRACTIONS

Budai Vár (Buda Castle)

Also known as the Royal Palace, Buda Castle is actually a grouping of several structures built and rebuilt over the centuries, after successive conflicts with the Turks, the Habsburgs and the Germans. The first castle was constructed around 1255, but was reconstructed by King Matthias in 1458. During the Renaissance, the castle was at its architectural peak, featuring indoor plumbing and wine flowing from its fountains. All of this was destroyed during the Turkish siege of 1541. Reconstructed yet again after World War II, the castle now houses the Budapest History Museum and the Hungarian National Gallery (see page 69).

Budavári Sikló (Buda Castle Funicular)

First opened in 1870, this funicular railway was destroyed by the Germans in World War II. Lovingly restored in 1986, it continues to

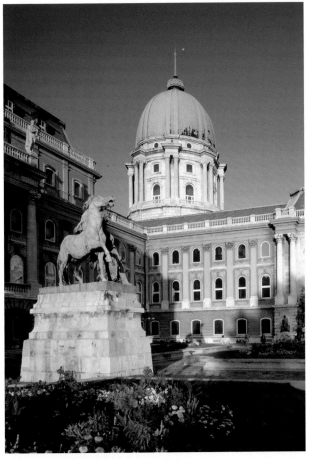

◐ *Buda Castle, also known as the Royal Palace*

haul intrepid passengers from Clark Ádám tér up to Buda Castle. You will get a great view of Pest and the Danube as you gain altitude.

Citadella (Citadel)

On St Stephen's Day (20 August), the Hungarian army sets fireworks ablaze from this monument built by the Habsburgs after the 1848–9 uprising. Constructed to intimidate Budapesters, today it houses a youth hostel and nightclub, testament to the power that reigns over modern-day Budapest: tourism. ⓦ www.citadella.hu

Felszabadulási Emlékmű (Liberation Monument)

This controversial statue of Lady Liberty perched atop the Citadel is one of the few remaining pieces of Soviet public art in Budapest. Originally commissioned to commemorate the 'liberation' of Budapest by Soviet forces, it now honours all those who 'laid down their lives for Hungarian prosperity'.

Gellért Emlékmű (Gellért Monument)

This monument was erected in 1904 to atone for the sins of the fathers of Budapest, who, to renounce the Christian faith, pushed Bishop Gellért over the hill in a spiked barrel. Lit up at night, it's a beautiful beacon. ⓝ Tram: 18, 19

Halászbástya (Fishermen's Bastion)

A statue of St Stephen guards this neo-Romanesque structure. The view is stunning, especially in the early morning or late evening when the tourist hordes have diminished. It was built in 1895 as a monument to the Fishermen's Guild. ⓛ 09.00–23.00

◗ *The Buda Castle Funicular climbs above the city*

Mátyás Templom (Matthias Church)

It's interesting to note that although the Hungarian King Matthias lent his name to this church built in 1470, Hungarians were not permitted to worship here. Germans worshipped at the church until the Turks came to power and converted it into a mosque. Legend has it that, in 1686, a vision of the Madonna appeared during prayers at the mosque. The Turks took the hint, and lost the city to the Habsburgs. **ⓐ** I. Szentháromság tér 2 **ⓣ** (1) 355 5657 **ⓦ** www.matyas-templom.hu **ⓛ** 09.00–17.00 Mon–Fri, 09.00–12.00 Sat, 13.00–17.00 Sun. Admission charge (but not to under-sixes)

Sándor Palota (Alexander Palace)

This is the home of the Hungarian president. Unless you are on official business, you can't see the beauty that lies within. However, you can admire its neoclassical façade reconstructed after World War II. **ⓐ** I. Szent György tér 1

Sziklatemplom (Cave Church)

This church set in the cliffside was founded by Pauline monks in 1926. In the 1950s, the Communists put a stop to their Order, murdering the leader and sentencing the rest of the monks to prison. The church was bricked up and forgotten until August 1989, after the fall of the Communist regime. The result is a spooky and strange house of worship, but worth the visit. **ⓐ** XI. Gellérthegy **ⓛ** 09.00–11.00, 12.00–16.00, 18.30–19.30 **ⓝ** Tram: 7, 19, 47

Úri utca (Lords' Street)

Medieval-styled façades of houses built after the 1950s give this street, perfect for strolling, its special character. Highlights include no. 9, where the Buda Castle Labyrinth begins, no. 31 with Gothic ornamentation and no. 49, which houses the **Telephone Museum** (see Ⓦ www.budapestinfo.hu for information on opening hours).

CULTURE

Arany Sas Patikamúzeum (Golden Eagle Pharmaceutical Museum)

One of the oldest houses in the Castle District, this museum holds interesting exhibits of Hungarian pharmaceutical history, including an alchemical laboratory. It even has mummy powder from Transylvania. ⓐ I. Tárnok utca 18 ⓣ (1) 375 9772

Budapesti Történeti Múzeum (Budapest History Museum)

With artefacts, illustrations and photos of excavations, this museum traces the development of Budapest from the dawn of human history to the present day. Temporary rotating exhibitions fill out the experience nicely. ⓐ I. Szent György tér 2 Ⓦ www.btm.hu Ⓛ 10.00–16.00 Mon, Wed–Sun, closed Tues, Nov–Feb; 10.00–18.00 Mar–Oct

Budavári Labirintus (Buda Castle Labyrinth)

Used as an air-raid shelter during World War II, this network of caves and passageways houses a cheeky anti-art exhibition by Hungarian art students. The caves have been separated into chambers and halls, including the Renaissance Hall of Rocks with its novel ivy-covered fountain spouting red wine. ⓐ I. Úri utca 9 ⓣ (1) 212 0287 Ⓦ www.labirintus.com Ⓛ 09.30–19.00

Gellért Fürdő (Gellért Baths)

Renovated in 2007, these are the best-known and probably most luxurious baths in Budapest, with soaring columns, stained-glass

MAKING THE MOST OF THE TURKISH BATHS

All of these baths have one thing in common: the Turks. When the Turks took Buda Castle in 1541, Buda became a Muslim city, the churches were converted to mosques and the natural limestone hot springs were made into traditional Turkish bathhouses that remain to this day. Each bath in Budapest has its own personality and own set of bizarre rules, but the same general rules apply.

A general entrance fee is all you need to make the most of the bathing experience. There are a gazillion other items on the menu, but most likely you will only want a massage and not a turbomatic skin slough. You pay for your massage (always given by a member of the same sex) at the ticket counter, for which you'll be given a token that you will then give to the masseur. Remember to tell them you don't speak Hungarian, so that they'll call your name out in English, or wave to you when it's your turn. When you hand your ticket to the bath attendant, you will get a silly-looking little cloth to tie around your waist. Women get some sort of apron-like covering for their breasts, but seldom use it. The idea is to move between pools and sauna, alternating temperatures from scalding hot to downright freezing until you find the right place to relax. At the end of your stay, you can relax in a resting room, before you put your street clothes back on.

You should bring your own towels and soap. The pools have separate areas for men, women and families, but most have a non-segregated pool. Lockers are free or for a nominal fee and you can also pay extra for your own cabin. Note that if you stay under two hours, you will receive some money back.

Sampling the waters is the perfect way to indulge in a little bit of local culture. Bathing plays a big part in the Hungarian way of life and the thermal waters are said to ease all sorts of ailments, including arthritis and skin complaints. Go to W www.budapestspas.hu for more information about the Budapest bathing experience.

windows and an outdoor swimming pool with one of the world's first wave machines. Sit in the splendour of the Viennese-style café, remembering that we owe it to the Turks when we're sipping our espresso. ⓐ XI. Kelenhegyi út 4 ⓣ (1) 466 6166

Király Fürdő (King's Baths)
Opened in 1566 for the Ottoman governor, you'll bask in glory at the central dome towering over the baths, saunas and steam areas. ⓐ II. Fő utca 82–84 ⓣ (1) 201 3688 ⓛ Women only 07.00–17.00 Mon, Wed & Fri; Men only 09.00–19.00 Tues, Thur & Sat

Magyar Nemzeti Galéria (Hungarian National Gallery)
The best of Hungarian creative arts are in the sumptuous rooms of this gallery, which is as much a work of art as the pieces hung on its walls. With collections ranging from medieval to contemporary, perhaps the strongest collection is from the 19th-century Secessionist movement, which pushed the boundaries into controversial subjects and the avant garde. Admission to the permanent exhibitions is free. ⓐ I. Dísz tér 17 W www.mng.hu ⓛ 10.00–18.00 Tues–Sun, closed Mon

Rudas Fürdő (Rudas Baths)

These are Budapest's finest Turkish baths. After extensive renovations in 2005, the baths retain their glorious Ottoman flavour. Shafts of light cut through the dimness, as the domes and chambers reflect the chatter of bathers and water lightly splashing. ⓐ I. Döbrentei tér 9 ⓣ (1) 356 1322 ⓛ Women only 06.00–19.00 Tues; Men only 06.00–19.00 Mon, Wed, Thur & Fri; mixed 06.00–16.00 Sat & Sun

RETAIL THERAPY

This area is not so much a shopping district as an atmospheric, impulse-buy district. For serious shopping, or on a rainy day, go to **Mammut** (ⓐ II. Lövőház utca 2–6 ⓣ (1) 345 8020 or 345 8333 ⓦ www.mammut.hu), a massive complex in Buda that not only houses more than 300 top-name fashion shops, but also has internet access, bowling, casinos, amusement arcades, cinemas, dance clubs and fitness studios. Gastronomes will appreciate the stylish restaurants and cafés in the surrounding area.

Auguszt Cukrászda A quaint family-owned business that just happens to supply some of the best cakes in town. ⓐ I. Fény utca 8 ⓣ (1) 316 3817 ⓛ 10.00–18.00 Tues–Fri, 09.00–18.00 Sat, closed Sun & Mon ⓝ Metro: Moszkva tér

Budapest Wine Society This is the place to sample the best local Hungarian wines. They stock hundreds of varieties, including rare and special vintages. ⓐ I. Batthyány utca 59 ⓦ www.bortarsasag.hu ⓛ 10.00–20.00 Mon–Fri, 10.00–18.00 Sat, closed Sun ⓝ Metro: Moszkva tér

Litea Bookshop and Tea Room Serving coffee, tea and good reads, this shop stocks a wide range of Hungarian books, CDs, guides, maps and postcards. ❸ I. Hess András tér 4 ❶ (1) 375 6987 ❼ www.litea.hu ❶ 10.00–18.00 ❽ Metro: Moszkva tér, then Várbusz to Castle Hill

Opal Art This upmarket glass shop favours contemporary and art nouveau designs. ❸ I. Hess András tér 4 ❶ 10.00–17.00 ❽ Metro: Moszkva tér, then Várbusz to Castle Hill

TAKING A BREAK

Café Gusto £ ❶ Serves great coffees, light salads and filling Hungarian specialities in this tucked-away spot near Margit híd (Margaret Bridge).

🔻 *Pick out a special bottle to take home*

⒜ I. Frankel Leó utca 12 ⓣ (1) 316 3970 ⓒ 10.00–22.00 Mon–Fri,
10.00–16.00 Sat, closed Sun

Miró Café £ ❷ A perfect stop for coffee and light snacks on quirky
Úri utca, boasting an interior inspired by the works of Catalan artist
Joan Miró. ⒜ I. Úri utca 30 ⓣ (1) 201 5573 ⓒ 09.00–00.00

⬤ *There are plenty of cosy coffee houses in Buda*

Ruszwurm £ ❸ Made famous not only for its great cakes served since 1827, but for its warm European styling, with finely crafted period furniture. ❷ I. Szentháromság utca 7, off Úri utca ❶ (1) 375 5284 ❹ 10.00–18.00

Soho Café £ ❹ A lovely location for a cuppa. ❷ I. Fő utca 25 ❶ (1) 201 3807 ❹ 08.00–21.00 Mon–Fri, 09.00–21.00 Sat & Sun

AFTER DARK

Buda is known for its upmarket dining establishments located on leafy side streets with exquisite views. For a livelier bar-and-club scene, you'll need to cross the Danube.

RESTAURANTS

Náncsi Néni £ ❺ A family-style restaurant, 'Aunt Nancy's' offers great Hungarian home cooking, live accordion music and free champagne for couples. A must to book ahead. ❷ II. Ördögárok utca 80 ❶ (1) 397 2742 ❹ 12.00–23.00 Mon–Fri, 09.00–23.00 Sat & Sun ❿ Tram: 56

Aranyszarvas ££ ❻ If you're game for game, this is the place for you. ❷ I. Szarvas tér 1 ❶ (1) 375 6451 ❹ 12.00–23.00

Café Pierrot ££ ❼ An intimate bistro serving international specialities and excellent pancakes late into the night. Piano music for that added atmosphere. ❷ I. Fortuna utca 14 ❶ (1) 375 6971 ❹ 11.00–00.00

Carne di Hall ££ ❽ With a name like this, you know it's a meat-eater's paradise. Also features an excellent selection of wines. ❷ I. Bem rakpart 20, off Fő utca ❶ (1) 201 8137 ❹12.00–00.00

Fortuna ££ ❾ Hungarian and international specialities on a leafy side street. ❸ I. Hess András tér 4 ☎ (1) 375 6857 ⌚ 19.00–00.00 Mon–Sat, closed Sun

Fuji Japanese Restaurant ££ ❿ For a landlocked country, the sushi is surprisingly good. ❸ II. Csatárka utca 54 ☎ (1) 325 7111 ⌚ 12.00–23.00

Malomtó ££ ⓫ Asian-inspired flavours close to the Lukács Baths. Get a seat outside on the lakeside terrace if you can. ❸ II. Frankel Leó utca 48 ☎ (1) 336 1830 ⌚ 12.00–00.00 Tues–Sun, closed Mon

Alabárdos £££ ⓬ Transylvanian specialities have a long history at this 40-year-old restaurant, set in a 400-year-old building. The menu features authentic Hungarian cuisine, and the outdoor terrace is a stunner in the summer. As expensive as it gets, but you're worth it. Reservations recommended. ❸ I. Országház utca 2 ☎ (1) 356 0851 ⓦ www.alabardos.hu ⌚ 12.00–16.00, 19.00–23.00 Mon–Sat, closed Sun ⓝ Metro: Moszkva tér, then Várbusz to Castle Hill

Arany Kaviár £££ ⓭ Russian cuisine at its finest. ❸ I. Ostrom utca 19 ☎ (1) 201 6737 ⌚ 12.00–00.00

Rivalda Restaurant £££ ⓮ Modern fusion Hungarian presented with impeccable service. Find out why this restaurant has consistently been voted the best restaurant in Budapest by a number of reviewers. Reservations recommended. ❸ I. Színház utca 5–9, off Úri utca ☎ (1) 489 0236 ⌚ 11.30–23.30

▶ *There are stunning views from the cafés on Fishermen's Bastion*

BARS & CLUBS

A38 A moored Ukrainian party barge, featuring three floors to suit different tastes. Fab bands play on the lower deck; the middle deck offers a chilled-out restaurant and bar; the top deck grooves to excellent dance tunes. ⓐ XI. Pázmány Péter rakpart ⓣ (1) 464 3940 ⓦ www.a38.hu ⓛ 12.00–04.00 ⓝ Tram: 4 or 6; metro: Boráros tér, then cross the bridge

Jam Pub Situated in the Mammut shopping centre (see page 70), this is a popular bar and pub, with live music every day. Serves great soup in bread loaves. ⓐ II. Lövőház utca 1–3 ⓣ (1) 345 8301 ⓦ www.jampub.hu ⓛ 08.00–04.00 Sun–Wed, 08.00–06.00 Thurs–Sat ⓝ Metro: Moszkva tér

Kaméleon Klub Also in the Mammut shopping centre, this club stomps Buda with Latin and jazz beats until dawn. The crowd is an unpretentious mix of locals and expats, the interior is kitschedelic, and you can't help but have a great time. ⓐ II. Lövőház utca 1–5 ⓣ (1) 345 8547 ⓛ 20.00–05.00 ⓝ Metro: Moszkva tér

Libella Not far from Szent Gellért tér is a homely oasis serving some of the best beer in Buda. In the late hours, a mix of geeky engineering students, old diehards playing cards and sports fans watching the TV makes for an intriguing night out. ⓐ XI. Budafoki út 7 ⓣ (1) 209 4761 ⓛ 08.00–01.00 Mon–Fri, 10.00–01.00 Sat, 12.00–01.00 Sun ⓝ Tram: 18, 47, 49

ⓞ *Floodlit Buda Castle towers over the Danube*

Pest: around Parliament

Pest is the true heart of the city, where people go about their daily lives. While the other side of the Danube was getting richer in the 19th century, factory workers, builders, shopkeepers and their families set up shop in Pest, making this a wholly Magyar metropolis. It quickly flourished, setting the stage for even greater expansion of Hungarian cultural pursuits, further stirring the stew that would lead to revolution.

At the end of the 19th century, Budapest's burgeoning population got down to business, making Budapest a world city. Nowhere is this more apparent than around the Parliament building, where grand boulevards, large squares and triumphant architecture house cultural treasures, high-end hotels and some of the best restaurants in Budapest.

Pest has seen some of the worst atrocities of the 20th century, and though the bullet holes are still visible in many façades, the municipality is committed to cleaning up the city with more green spaces and less traffic. The scars can stay. Hungarians prefer not to forget.

SIGHTS & ATTRACTIONS

Kossuth Lajos tér (Lajos Kossuth Square)

Named after the man who led the 1848–9 uprising against the Habsburgs, this square has splendid monuments paying tribute to Hungarian revolts against Austrian and later Soviet oppression.
Ⓝ Metro: Kossuth Lajos tér

Országház (Houses of Parliament)

White neo-Gothic turrets and arches inspired by the Palace of Westminster stretch magnificently along the Danube. Inside, the impressive decoration, rich in Hungarian touches, winds its

● *The Houses of Parliament stretch elegantly along the Danube*

way down 20 km (12½ miles) of corridors. Take a quick 20–30 minute
tour of the chambers when Parliament is not in session, and sit on the
members' benches. Also on view is the holy crown, given to St Stephen
by the Pope in AD 1000 to commemorate Hungary's official inclusion
in the Christian faith. The 2006 demonstrations took place on the
grassed area in front of the building; it's here that protestors
against Soviet occupation were shot in 1956, sparking the revolution.
ⓐ V. Kossuth Lajos tér ⓣ (1) 441 4415 ⓛ 10.00–18.00 Tues–Sun, closed
Mon ⓜ Metro: Kossuth Lajos tér; tram: 2

Postatakarék Pénztár (Postal Savings Bank)

Designed in 1901 by Ödön Lechner, Hungary's answer to Gaudí, this
former postal savings bank is a stunning example of art nouveau
architecture. Tours of the inside of the building are given only once a
year, in May. ⓐ V. Hold utca 4 ⓣ (1) 428 2600 ⓜ Metro: Arany János utca

Roosevelt tér (Roosevelt Square)

At the head of the Lánchíd (Chain Bridge), this square's name has changed from 'Unloading Square' and 'Franz Josef's Square' to the current 'Roosevelt Square'. From the look of the hotels nearby, it could easily change its name again to 'Ritz Square'. Ⓜ Metro: Kossuth Lajos tér

Szabadság tér (Liberty Square)

Laid out in 1886 on the site of an Austrian soldiers' barracks, this square has long been a symbol of Hungary's struggle for independence. The Soviet war memorial that stands here is one of the few remaining works of socialist art left in Budapest, and remains to honour the sacrifices made by Red Army troops who died liberating Budapest in 1944–5. Ⓜ Metro: Kossuth Lajos tér

Városnéző Ballon (Sightseeing Balloon)

Extreme sightseeing as you waft some 150 m (500 ft) above the city for 15 minutes. On a hot day, it's the coolest way to get your bearings in the city. The balloon is attached by a metal cable above Nyugati pu, so don't worry about never making it back home. ❸ Westend City Center, Váci út 1–3 ❶ (1) 238 7623 Ⓜ Metro: Nyugati pu. Admission charges: adults, 3,000 HUF; children aged six to twelve, 2,000 HUF; children aged three to six, 1,000 HUF; free for those under three

CULTURE

Állami Operaház (State Opera House)

Designed by Miklós Ybl, the same architect who worked on St Stephen's Basilica (see page 84), this building is one of the finest historical buildings in town. Its walls feature 16 of the world's greatest composers, including Monteverdi, Mozart, Beethoven, Verdi, Bizet and Tchaikovsky.

🔺 *The magnificent State Opera House*

Inside, more than 7 kg (15 lb) of gold was used to decorate the horseshoe-shaped auditorium, which seats over 1,200 people. This venue features performances of ballet, classical music and opera nearly every day of the week. Even if you're not artistically inclined, just have a look at its amazing interior, and you may be persuaded to stay for a show. ⓐ VI. Andrássy út 22 ⓣ (1) 353 0170 ⓦ www.opera.hu ⓛ Box office 10.00–19.00, Guided tours 15.00 & 16.00 ⓜ Metro: Opera

Gresham Palota (Gresham Palace)
John Gresham never set foot in Budapest. His building was commissioned 300 years after his death in 1904 by the Gresham

Life Assurance Company of London. If he was alive today, he would be pleased with the results. After its completion in 1906, it was the most modern building of the time, fitted out with all the latest amenities, including central heating and a unique central vacuum system. Though damaged in both World War II and the 1956 revolution, the beautiful wrought-iron peacock entrance gates survived intact. Now, it is part of the Four Seasons Hotel chain, and houses a wonderful coffee house where you can ponder its history in style. ⓐ V. Roosevelt tér 6 ⓘ (1) 268 6000 ⓦ www.greshampalace.com ⓛ Variable: phone to arrange a visit ⓝ Metro: Vörösmarty tér

Néprajzi Múzeum (Ethnographic Museum)

The grand location opposite Parliament makes it safe to assume that Hungarians take their culture seriously. A huge entrance hall, with chandeliers and marble staircases, leads to colourfully exhibited costumes, toys, objects associated with weddings and funerals, and depictions of village and farm life. Admission is free, and all information is in English. ⓐ V. Kossuth Lajos tér 12 ⓘ (1) 473 2400 ⓦ www.neprajz.hu ⓛ 09.00–17.00 Mon–Sat, closed Sun ⓝ Metro: Kossuth Lajos tér

RETAIL THERAPY

It's an expensive undertaking to shop in this district, filled with quality antique items and one-of-a-kind finds. If you're looking for that special something, this may be the place for you.

Bestsellers Home from home for expats, offering the best in English-language literature. ⓐ V. Október 6 utca 11 ⓘ (1) 312 1295 ⓛ 09.00–18.30 Mon–Fri, 10.00–17.00 Sat, 10.00–16.00 Sun ⓝ Metro: Arany János utca

THE CITY

SZENT ISTVÁN BAZILIKA (ST STEPHEN'S BASILICA)

A must-see for any visitor to Budapest, St Stephen's Basilica is Budapest's largest church and is identical in height to Parliament. It's perfect now, but wasn't always that way. After the original dome fell, famous Hungarian architect Miklós Ybl set to work repairing his architectural predecessor's mistakes. Although it suffered damage from bombings in World War II, the church has remained standing thanks to Ybl's sounder, neo-Renaissance design. In the Szent jobb kápolna (Chapel of the Sacred Right) lies Catholic Hungary's most revered and creepy relic – what is claimed to be the mummified right hand of St Stephen. Improvements on the interior include additional lighting in the nave for appreciating all the works of art and sculptures within, and a complete renovation of the organ. @ V. Szent István tér 33 ☎ (1) 317 2859 ⓦ www.basilica.hu ◷ 09.00–17.00 Ⓜ Metro: Arany János utca or Bajcsy-Zsilinszky út

Eclectick Design Shop A respite from the usual high-street designs, this is the place to pick up funky Hungarian threads. @ V. Irányi utca 20 ☎ (1) 266 3341 ⓦ www.eclectick.hu ◷ 10.00–19.00 Mon–Fri, 11.00–16.00 Sat, closed Sun Ⓣ Tram: 4, 6

Girardi Kalapház Haute hats made with Hungarian haberdashery. @ XIII. Szent István körút 26 ☎ (1) 376 5376 ◷ 10.00–17.30 Mon–Fri, closed Sat & Sun Ⓜ Metro: Nyugati pu

Orlando Collection Haute couture meets the street in wonderful prêt-à-porter by young Hungarian designers. @ V. Zoltán utca 11

🔺 *St Stephen's Basilica is Budapest's largest church*

(1) 311 8242 🕙 10.00–18.00 Mon–Fri, 10.00–13.00 Sat, closed Sun
🅝 Metro: Kossuth Lajos tér

Pintér Antik Housed in what used to be an air-raid shelter, this large,
flaunty antiques shop serves coffee as well. Good for lubricating the
purse strings. 🅐 V. Falk Miksa utca 10 ⓣ (1) 311 3030 🕙 10.00–18.00
Mon–Fri, 10.00–14.00 Sat, closed Sun 🅝 Metro: Kossuth Lajos tér

Vasseva Clothing, bedding and accessories with a thoroughly modern
and minimalist touch. 🅐 VI. Paulay Ede utca 67 ⓣ (1) 342 8159
🕙 12.00–20.00 Mon–Fri, closed Sat & Sun 🅝 Metro: Opera

Virág Judit Galéria és Aukciósház An excellent collection of antique
paintings and porcelain. 🅐 V. Falk Miksa utca 30 ⓣ (1) 312 2071 🕙 10.00–
18.00 Mon–Fri, 10.00–13.00 Sat, closed Sun 🅝 Metro: Kossuth Lajos tér

Westend City Center This shopping centre, polished, pristine and
usually packed with people, features more than 400 upmarket shops,
cinemas, amusement arcades and even a sightseeing balloon. You
won't find a bargain here, but you may find some fun, especially
when the temperatures soar or the weather is uncooperative.
🅐 VI. Váci út 1–3 ⓣ (1) 238 7777 🅦 www.westend.hu 🕙 08.00–23.00
Mon–Sat, 08.00–22.00 Sun 🅝 Metro: Nyugati pu

TAKING A BREAK

Balettcipő £ ❶ 'Ballet Shoes' will keep you on your toes, with a long
list of coffees, cocktails and even some salads. 🅐 VI. Hajós utca 14
ⓣ (1) 269 3114 🕙 09.00–00.00 Mon–Fri, 11.00–00.00 Sat & Sun
🅝 Metro: Opera

Beckett's £ ❷ The friendly, informal centre of Budapest's expat scene. It definitely serves the best pub grub in the city, and there's Guinness on tap. ⓐ V. Bajcsy-Zsilinszky út 72 ❶ (1) 311 1035 ❻ 12.00–01.00 Mon–Fri & Sun, 12.00–02.00 Sat ⓝ Metro: Nyugati pu

Café Bouchon £ ❸ A popular restaurant serving international dishes in an unpretentious setting – get there early for a seat. ⓐ VI. Zichy Jenő utca 33 ❶ (1) 353 4094 ⓦ www.cafebouchon.hu ❻ 09.00–23.00 Mon–Sat, closed Sun

Café Kör £ ❹ Sample some national cuisine in this cosy Hungarian café with an appropriate name! ⓐ V. Sas utca 17 ❶ (1) 311 0053 ❻ 10.00–22.00 Mon–Sat, closed Sun ⓝ Metro: Arany János utca

Centrál Kávéház £ ❺ This place has reinvented itself, but remains an old-fashioned watering hole for intellectuals, travellers and Budapesters in the know. Also serves excellent meals at a reasonable price. Not bad for its location. ⓐ V. Károlyi Mihály utca 9 ❶ (1) 266 2110 ❻ 08.00–00.00 ⓝ Metro: Ferenciek tere

Gerbeaud £ ❻ The place to get fuelled on gooey Hungarian and Viennese sweets and hot chocolate that's literally just melted milk chocolate. The interior is as lovely as what's in the display case; unfortunately, service sometimes isn't. Try your luck. ⓐ V. Vörösmarty tér 7 ❶ (1) 429 9000 ❻ 09.00–21.00 ⓝ Metro: Vörösmarty tér

Java Café £ ❼ This small, Starbucks-like café with a tourist and local clientele is close to Parliament. Great cakes, muffins and sandwiches. ⓐ V. Aulich utca 7 ❶ (1) 311 2251 ❻ 07.00–19.00 Mon–Fri, 09.00–14.00 Sat, closed Sun ⓝ Metro: Kossuth Lajos tér

AFTER DARK

RESTAURANTS

Ba Bar £ ❽ Chic and sleek, the vibe is lingering Mediterranean, and so is the food. Excellent mixed drinks and wine list will keep you after hours. ❸ VII. Huszár utca 7 🕐 11.30–01.00 Mon–Thur, 11.30–02.00 Fri & Sat, closed Sun Ⓜ Metro: Keleti pu

Govinda £ ❾ A simple establishment serving wonderfully filling vegetarian dishes. ❸ V. Vigyázó Ferenc utca 4, off Oktober 6 utca ☎ (1) 269 1625 🕐 12.00–21.00 Ⓜ Metro: Arany János utca

Momotaro Ramen £ ❿ A mixture of Chinese and Japanese, but the outcome is tasty. You won't linger, as the seating isn't too comfortable, but you will leave happy and full. ❸ V. Széchenyi utca 16 ☎ (1) 269 3802 🕐 11.00–22.00 Ⓜ Metro: Kossuth Lajos tér

Dió Restaurant ££ ⓫ Trendy Hungarian restaurant serving contemporary dishes. ❸ V. Sas utca 4 ☎ (1) 3280360 🔵 www.diorestaurant.com 🕐 12.00–00.00 Ⓜ Metro: Arany János utca

Tom George Restaurant and Café ££ ⓬ Serves Hungarian and Oriental fusion in a self-consciously trendy setting. ❸ V. Oktober 6 utca 8 ☎ (1) 266 3525 🕐 12.00–00.00 Mon–Fri, 12.00–01.00 Sat & Sun Ⓜ Metro: Vörösmarty tér

Páva £££ ⓭ Housed in the Gresham Palace, with a view of the Chain Bridge, this is one of the best-known (and, surprisingly, not one of the most expensive) restaurants in Budapest. A 5-star performance from start to finish, and make sure you save room for the wonderful desserts.

Reservations recommended. ⓐ V. Roosevelt tér 5–6 ① (1) 268 600 ⓛ 18.00–22.30 Mon–Sat, closed Sun ⓝ Metro: Vörösmarty tér

BARS & CLUBS

Columbus Pub & Jazz Club This moored party boat serves light food and coffee all day and is a favourite with families who come here for lunch. At night, the mood swings, and tables are used for dancing. ⓐ V. Vigadó tér 4 ① (1) 266 9013 ⓛ 12.00–00.00 ⓝ Metro: Vörösmarty tér

Fat Mo's An American-style basement bar with great bands and great steaks. ⓐ V. Nyáry Pál utca 11 ① (1) 267 3199 ⓦ www.fatmo.hu ⓛ 12.00–02.00 Mon–Wed, 12.00–04.00 Thur & Fri, 18.00–04.00 Sat, 18.00–02.00 Sun ⓝ Metro: Kálvin tér

Merlin Theatre The place to cut a rug with an eclectic crowd. ⓐ V. Gerlóczy utca 4 ① (1) 317 9338 ⓦ www.merlinszinhaz.hu ⓛ 12.00–00.10 ⓝ Metro: Ferenciek tere

Morrisons Music Pub A buzzing music pub – not exactly swish but has a great atmosphere. ⓐ V. Honvéd utca 40 ① (1) 374 3329 ⓦ www.morrisons.hu ⓛ 17.00–04.00 Mon–Sat, closed Sun ⓝ Metro: Nyugati pu

Trafó Bár Tangó The place to mingle with bright young Budapesters. ⓐ IX. Liliom utca 41 ① (1) 456 2040 ⓦ www.trafo.hu ⓛ 18.00–04.00 ⓝ Metro: Ferenc körút

Tulipán Presszó A bar that never sleeps, so bring your cards and join the insomniac locals and tourists. ⓐ V. Nádor utca 34 ① (1) 269 5043 ⓛ 24 hours ⓝ Metro: Kossuth Lajos tér

Central Pest & the Városliget

In Budapest, all roads lead to Váci utca. It's no wonder: this was once the main road to the city, and now this pedestrian-only thoroughfare is filled with chic cafés, upmarket boutiques and speciality shops. Window shopping and people-watching are the favoured activities, and sitting at an outdoor café, enjoying the flow of locals and tourists alike, is one of the primary pleasures.

From Váci utca, walking northeast, along Pest's most beautiful street, Andrássy út, you'll encounter more of what makes this city wonderful: its commitment to making movement pleasurable. You will follow rows of apartment buildings, walk past theatres and reach a leafy diplomatic quarter, where the boulevards become quieter and more picturesque. Running just beneath the street is the Metró, the first underground line in continental Europe. When you make your way to the Városliget (City Park, see page 93), the space and fresh air will intoxicate you.

At night, you can fill up your lungs again in many of the cafés, clubs and bars that surround Liszt Ferenc tér (Franz Liszt Square), close to the Oktogon metro station if you need to make a quick getaway.

For a wonderfully unique evening out, keep an eye out for posters scattered around Pest with the word '*kert*' scribbled on. This literally translates into 'garden' but *kerts* in a socialising sense are essentially bars squatting in old buildings that may or may not be crumbling around your ears. Locals young and old will hang out in these *kerts*, where the drinks are cheap and food is often simple soups or rolls. Unfortunately, some of these *kerts* shut down during the winter months and may or may not open up in the same spot, meaning you have to rediscover your favourite drinking hole when the city thaws.

An institution in the city is a *kert* called **Szimpla** (🌐 www.szimpla.hu), and its website sums up *kert*dom beautifully.

SIGHTS & ATTRACTIONS

Belvárosi Főplébániatemplom (Inner City Parish Church)
This is the oldest building in Pest. Originally a 12th-century Romanesque church, it has survived the ravages of Mongols and Turks. In the 16th century it was converted into a mosque, and after World War II the church was again threatened, this time by the Hungarian authorities who planned to demolish it in order to rebuild Erzsébet híd (Elizabeth Bridge). As you can see, the bridge was skilfully re-routed around the church. Behind the high altar, you'll find an amazingly intact Turkish prayer niche. 🅰 V. Március 15. tér 2 ☎ (1) 318 3108 🕐 08.00–19.00 Ⓜ Metro: Ferenciek tere

Deák tér Evangélikus Templom (Deák Square Lutheran Church)
Built in 1809, this building originally housed military uniforms. A couple of years later, it became a Protestant church, quite radical for the times. This building is unique in its Protestant lack of ornamentation. The church can be seen during services (🅰 V. Deák tér 5 🕐 10.00–18.00 Tues–Sun, closed Mon). It can also be seen as part of a visit to the next-door **National Lutheran Museum** (🅰 V. Deák tér 4 ☎ (1) 317 4173 🌐 www.lutheran.hu 🕐 10.00–18.00 Tues–Sun, closed Mon Ⓜ Metro: Deák Ferenc tér).

Ferences Templom (Franciscan Church)
This 13th-century church was, like many of the other churches in Budapest, converted into a mosque during the Turkish occupation of the 16th and 17th centuries. Rebuilt by Franciscan monks in the late 18th

century, the façade and baroque altar are remarkable. ⓐ V. Ferenciek tere 9 ⓘ (1) 317 3322 ⓛ 07.00–19.00 Ⓝ Metro: Ferenciek tere

Hősök tere (Heroes' Square)

This square was once the place for anti-communist demonstrations. Now its grand expanse and perfect glassy surface is appreciated by skateboarders and BMX stunt punters. The Millennium Monument here was erected in 1896 to commemorate the 1,000th anniversary of the Hungarians' settlement of the Carpathian Basin. Standing on top of a column is the Archangel Gabriel, who appeared to St Stephen in a dream and offered him the crown of Hungary. The 'seven chieftains' sit at the foot of the column, representing the seven Magyar tribes who settled in Hungary in the 9th century. Ⓝ Metro: Hősök tere

Szerb Templom (Serbian Church)

Built in the baroque style by Serbian settlers in 1698, the church functions according to Greek Orthodox tradition: a wooden railing separates the women's and men's areas, and an iconostasis surrounds the gallery to keep all the churchgoers in line. ⓐ V. Szerb utca 2–4 ⓛ 08.00–19.00 Ⓝ Metro: Ferenciek tere or Kálvin tér

Városliget (City Park)

Once unusable swampland, this is now Budapest's largest park, offering something for everyone. The most imposing building is Vajdahunyad vára (Vajdahunyad Castle), a hotchpotch of architectural styles (Romanesque, Gothic, Renaissance and baroque) designed to represent more than 20 famous Hungarian buildings. The only area of the castle open to the public is the **Museum of Agriculture** (ⓘ (1) 363 1973 ⓛ 10.00–16.00), which has an interesting exhibition about Hungarian wine-making. In winter, the artificial

lake turns into a vast skating rink. Other attractions in the Városliget include the Széchenyi Baths (see page 46). The **Petőfi Csarnok** (🅦 www.petoficsarnok.hu), a concert venue, is also located here.
🅝 Metro: Hősök tere

CULTURE

Hopp Ferenc Kelet-Ázsiai Múzeum (Ferenc Hopp Museum of East Asian Art)

When Hungarian businessman Ferenc Hopp died in 1919, he left behind over 20,000 objects from India and the Far East. Ancient Buddhist art is shown alongside Japanese, Indian and Tibetan–Nepalese pieces. 🅐 VI. Andrássy út 103 🅣 (1) 322 8476 🅦 www.hoppmuzeum.hu 🅛 10.00–16.00 Tues–Sun, closed Mon 🅝 Metro: Bajza utca. Admission charge (except national holidays)

Merlin Színház (Merlin Theatre)

This is the only theatre in Budapest that offers regular performances in English. Evocative performers make shows contemporary and thought-provoking. There's also a bar for hanging out and musing with other thespians. 🅐 V. Gerlóczy utca 4 🅣 (1) 317 9338 🅝 Metro: Astoria, Deák Ferenc tér or Ferenciek tere

Szépművészeti Múzeum (Museum of Fine Arts)

This museum houses an important collection of non-Hungarian art, with items dating from the Egyptian era to the present, and galleries that are home to famous works by El Greco, Goya, Rembrandt and Rubens. Exciting temporary exhibitions are also worth a visit. 🅐 XIV. Hősök tere 🅣 (1) 469 7100 🅦 www.szepmuveszeti.hu 🅛 10.30–17.30 Tues–Sun, closed Mon 🅝 Metro: Hősök tere

BUDAPEST'S JEWISH QUARTER

By 1910, there were more than 200,000 Jews in Budapest, making up nearly 25 per cent of the city's population. Forbidden to live within the city walls, they lived in a quarter bordered by Andrássy út and Rákóczi út in the VII. district. During the 1848 uprising, Jews stood against the Habsburgs with their fellow Budapesters. By 1867, they obtained legal equality, thereby attracting an immigration of Jews from surrounding countries. Jewish businesses boomed, which helped Budapest on its way to becoming a great financial centre. During the 1930s and 1940s, Budapest Jews suffered pressure from right-wing government campaigns, followed by fascist ideologies that would wall them off into a ghetto within the capital. World War II saw the loss of some 700,000 Hungarian Jews, but the Budapest ghetto, established within the confines of the old Jewish quarter, was the only ghetto in Europe that wasn't completely destroyed. Here, the arrival of the Red Army really did mean liberation. Today, more than 3,000 Orthodox Jews live in the Jewish quarter, where you can find many Orthodox synagogues built in protest against the Great Synagogue, which some clerics argue is too close to Christianity for comfort. Besides synagogues, you'll find kosher markets, and get a feeling for Jewish neighbourhood life. The following will provide an enhanced understanding of this unforgettable part of the city:

Jewish Quarter Walking Tours Perfect to learn more about the Jewish tradition in Budapest. Tours leave from the Great Synagogue (see page 96). Admission is 5,900 HUF for a 2¹/₂-hour tour that also takes in the synagogue, with an opportunity to eat kosher food along the way or 3,300 HUF for a 60-minute walk around the quarter. 🚋 VII. Dohány utca 2 📞 (1) 317 2754 🌐 www.greatsynagogue.hu 🕐 Tours depart 10.30, 13.30 Mon–Thur, 10.30 Fri, 11.30 Sun Ⓜ Metro: Astoria

Magyar Zsidó Múzeum (Hungarian Jewish Museum)
Established in 1931, this museum houses Jewish relics from the 18th and 19th centuries, from both Hungary and abroad, grouped according to religious significance. The exhibition ends with moving photo and press documentation of the insanity of the Holocaust in Hungary. The museum stands where Theodor Herzl (1860–1904), the father of Zionism, was born. 🚋 VII. Dohány utca 2 📞 (1) 343 6756 🕐 10.00–17.00 Mon–Thur, 10.00–14.00 Fri &Sun, closed Sat Ⓜ Metro: Astoria

Nagy Zsinagóga (Great Synagogue) This synagogue is the second-largest in the world. Completed in 1859, its onion domes and façades are Byzantine-inspired. The design also expresses 19th-century Hungarian Jews' aspirations to assimilate, with twin towers that look like church steeples, and an organ chamber. Germans turned the synagogue into a detention camp in World War II; more than 3,000 Jews who didn't survive were buried in mass graves in the courtyard. Admission to the Great Synagogue is 1,200 HUF and entitles you to visit the Hungarian Jewish Museum (see above) next door. 🚋 VII. Dohány utca 2 📞 (1) 317 2754 🌐 www.greatsynagogue.hu 🕐 10.00–17.00 Mon–Thur, 10.00–14.00 Fri & Sun, closed Sat Ⓜ Metro: Astoria

◗ Budapest's Great Synagogue is the second largest in the world

Terror Háza Múzeum (House of Terror Museum)

This controversial museum, built to commemorate the horrors that Hungary suffered under the two terror regimes of the Nazis and the Communists, opened its doors in 2002. For some, it's over the top; for others, a chilling reminder of what can happen if we get too complacent about world politics. The interrogation rooms, torture devices, propaganda samples and video clips of interviews with survivors from the 1956 revolution bring the points home.

ⓐ VI. Andrássy út 60 ⓣ (1) 374 2600 ⓦ www.terrorhaza.hu ⓛ 10.00–18.00 Mon–Fri, 10.00–19.30 Sat & Sun ⓝ Metro: Vörösmarty utca

RETAIL THERAPY

Folkart Centrum This is the largest folk-art shop in Hungary and offers a wide range of authentically handcrafted products from all over the country. Clothing, embroidery, homespun wool, handwoven articles, painted Easter eggs, porcelain, pottery, traditional flasks, wooden carvings and other small souvenir items make perfect gifts.
ⓐ Váci utca 58 ⓣ (1) 318 5840 ⓦ www.folkartcentrum.hu ⓛ 10.00–19.00 ⓝ Metro: Ferenciek tere

Louis Vuitton Situated in a prime piece of real estate, this is the place to pick up your genuine Vuitton luggage. ⓐ VI. Andrassy út 24 ⓣ (1) 373 0487 ⓛ 10.00–19.00 Mon–Fri, 11.00–18.00 Sat, closed Sun ⓝ Metro: Opera

Nagyvásárcsarnok (Great Market Hall) Situated on the Pest side of the Szabadság híd (Liberty Bridge), the Great Market Hall is a remarkable building that should not be missed, though the looming exterior is far more stunning that the cluttered interior (it was designed by Gustave Eiffel of Eiffel Tower fame). Make your way past tourists and

● *The Great Market Hall in Pest was designed by Gustave Eiffel*

grandmas buying ingredients for the evening goulash, and bask in the reality of it all. If reality becomes too much, in the basement a grocer sells all those things you miss from back home. ⓐ IX. Vámház körút 1–3 ① (1) 217 6067 ① 06.00–17.00 Mon–Fri, 06.00–14.00 Sat, closed Sun Ⓝ Metro: Kálvin tér

Párizsi udvar (Parisian Arcade) This sumptuous and elaborate arcade was completed in 1913, and originally housed the Inner City Savings Bank. It functions today as a shopping arcade. As you meander through the building, note the bee-inspired details (bees were a symbol of thrift) and the arched glass ceiling. ⓐ V. Ferenciek tere 10–11 Ⓝ Metro: Ferenciek tere

VÁCI UTCA: SHOP TILL YOU DROP

It's impossible to count the number of shops lining Váci utca, in Budapest's premier shopping district. Suffice to say that once you're there, you've arrived in shoppers' heaven. A stroll down this spendthrift thoroughfare takes you past swish boutiques, jewellers, perfumeries and art galleries. Thankfully, it's not all expensive or out of bounds for the more budget-conscious traveller. Radiating from the hub of Váci utca are smaller, lesser-known streets presenting you with a rush of bookshops, cafés, gourmet wine shops and world-famous, oddly affordable confectioners. There's something for everyone. Párizsi utca sweetens the deal with Szamos marzipan and ice cream; Fehérhajó utca sells healing minerals; the Csók Gallery on the corner of Pesti Barnabás utca sells works by modern Hungarian artists; and Kígyó utca is gradually turning into a street of fine Zsolnay porcelain, famous for it golds, greens and blues. The possibilities are endless, but you know your limit, and so does your credit-card company. Metro: Ferenciek tere

TAKING A BREAK

Astoria Café £ ❶ Elegant coffees, cakes and snacks in the high-ceilinged Hotel Astoria. V. Kossuth Lajos utca 19–21 (1) 889 2549 07.00–23.00 Metro: Astoria

Chagall £ ❷ Great sandwiches served with Czech beer and a touch of Chagall makes a winning combination. VI. Hajós utca 27 (1) 302 4614 09.00–00.00 Metro: Opera or Arany János utca

Kogart £ ❸ A gallery restaurant serving thoughtfully prepared dishes to meat-eaters and vegetarians alike. ⓐ VI. Andrássy út 112 ❶ (1) 354 3820 ❷ 10.00–18.00 ❸ Metro: Bajza utca

Mai Manó Kávézó £ ❹ Arty, very arty. More Czech beer among the displays of black-and-white photos. A moody, smoky environment inside; outdoors perfect for an alfresco coffee. ⓐ VI. Nagymező utca 20 ❶ (1) 269 5642 ❷ 10.00–01.00 ❸ Metro: Opera

Menza £ ❺ Great food in a retro setting makes this popular with students and tourists alike. Try the *lángos*, a Hungarian speciality. ⓐ VI. Liszt Ferenc tér 2 ❶ (1) 413 1482 ❷ 10.00–00.00 ❸ Metro: Oktogon

AFTER DARK

RESTAURANTS

Buena Vista £ ❻ Classy, with warm woods, and warmer Mediterranean flavours. The outdoor terrace is a must in the summer months. ⓐ VI. Liszt Ferenc tér 4–5 ❶ (1) 344 6303 ❷ 10.00–00.00 Mon–Fri, 11.00–00.00 Sat & Sun ❸ Metro: Oktogon

Articsóka ££ ❼ A sleek fusion restaurant. Sip local wine while sitting on the stylish roof terrace. ⓐ VI. Zichy Jenő utca 17 ❶ (1) 302 7757 ❻ www.articsoka.hu ❷ 12.00–00.00 ❸ Metro: Arany János utca

Bock Bistro ££ ❽ Situated in the Corinthia Grand Hotel Royal, treat yourself to a bottle or three of wine from the extensive wine list. ⓐ VII. Erzsébet körút 43–49 ❶ (1) 321 0340 ❻ www.bockbisztro.hu ❷ 12.00–00.00 Mon–Sat, closed Sun ❸ Metro: Blaha Lujza tér

🔺 *Soak in the atmosphere of Pest in one of its outdoor cafés*

Cotton Club ££ ❽ Chicago reinvented in Budapest with restaurant, smoking room and gambling den. ⓐ VI. Jókai utca 26 ☎ (1) 354 0886 🕐 12.00–23.00 Ⓜ Metro: Oktogon

Mandarin ££ ❿ A funky bar and restaurant serving Hungarian and international dishes. ⓐ VI. Ó utca 24–26 ☎ (1) 688 1696 ⓦ www.mandarinbar.hu 🕐 10.00–01.00 Mon–Fri, 12.00–01.00 Sat & Sun Ⓜ Metro: Arany János utca

Firkász ££ ⓫ A place where writers meet, pianists play and waiters serve grandmother-style cuisine. ⓐ XIII. Tátra utca 18 ⓣ (1) 450 1118 ⓦ www.firkaszetterem.hu ⓛ 12.00–00.00

Fülemüle ££ ⓬ Tasty, classy, non-kosher Jewish dishes. ⓐ VIII. Kőfaragó utca 5 ⓣ (1) 266 7974 ⓦ www.fulemule.hu ⓛ 12.00–22.00 Sun–Thurs, 12.00–23.00 Fri & Sat ⓝ Metro: Blaha Lujza tér

Klassz £££ ⓭ A very trendy and rather expensive restaurant – so exclusive, you can't even book a table. ⓐ VI. Andrássy út 41 ⓛ 11.30–23.00 ⓝ Metro: Arany János utca

Napfényes Ízek £££ ⓮ A fabulous vegetarian restaurant. ⓐ VII. Rózsa utca 39 ⓣ (1) 351 5649 ⓛ 10.00–23.00 Mon–Fri, 12.00–23.00 Sat & Sun

BARS & CLUBS
Champs Sport Pub Missing your football team? Champs has booths with private televisions. ⓐ VII. Dohány utca 20 ⓣ (1) 413 1655 ⓛ 12.00–02.00 ⓝ Metro: Blaha Lujza tér

Club 7 Bawdy cabaret and a long list of cocktails. ⓐ VII. Akácfa utca 7 ⓣ (1) 498 9030 ⓛ 10.00–05.00 ⓝ Metro: Blaha Lujza tér

Old Man's Music Club This is the place in Budapest to catch the blues. ⓐ VII. Akácfa utca 13 ⓣ (1) 322 7645 ⓦ www.oldmans.hu ⓛ 10.00–03.00 ⓝ Metro: Blaha Lujza tér

Szóda Café A laid-back bar with illustrations and original graphics adorning the walls and ceiling. ⓐ VII. Wesselényi utca 18 ⓣ (1) 461 0007 ⓦ www.szoda.com ⓛ 08.00–05.00 ⓝ Tram: 4, 6

Around Budapest

Though the city centre has enough to keep anyone busy for a
lifetime, Budapest is quickly sprawling out of its city limits, reaching
towards its ancient historical roots in Aquincum, or its prehistory
in the caves of the Buda Hills, blurring the distinction between
town and suburb. Places that were once a day trip have now been
connected by the HÉV, the suburban rail network that links central
Budapest with greater Budapest, as well as by more frequent and
convenient bus services.

   If you want to get your shoulders tanned in rugged nature or
breathe the air of Budapest's history, you should take at least one
quick jaunt to some of these sites. They're worth the effort, and
you'll make it back in time to dance on a few more tables before
your flight home.

SIGHTS & ATTRACTIONS

Aquincum Roman ruins

In the 2nd and 3rd centuries AD, Aquincum was the bustling capital
of the Roman province Pannonia, serving as a trading settlement
and garrison town. The excavated ruins give us a glimpse into
public and private life at the time. Highlights of the museum are
a reconstructed 3rd-century water organ, temporary exhibitions,
chronoscopes showing the original appearance of buildings, and
the small amphitheatre right next door. Ironically, the ruins sit
among the suburban sprawl of Budapest. ⓐ III. Szentendrei út 139
ⓦ www.aquincum.hu ⓛ 09.00–18.00 May–Sept; 09.00–17.00
Oct–Apr ⓥ HÉV: Aquincum

Budai hegyek (Buda Hills)

Head for the hills (in particular, Széchenyi hegy, Sváb hegy, János hegy and Hármashatár hegy)! From Fasor tér, take the *fogaskerekű-vasút* (cogwheel railway) or the *libegő* (chairlift) up to the top. A mecca for nature lovers, the Buda Hills (at around 400–500 m, or 1,300–1,600 ft, above sea level) lie to the northwest of the city centre, and offer clean air and endless woods with well-marked tourist trails. In addition to walking and cycling, the most popular means of getting around for tourists is the **Children's Railway** (Ⓦ www.gyermekvasut.com), a narrow-gauge railway that is operated by specially trained children. The **Budakeszi Wildlife Park** (Ⓣ (23) 451 783 Ⓦ www.vadaspark-budakeszi.hu) occupies more than 300 hectares (750 acres) of woodland, where you can see real Budapest party animals (of the boar and wolf persuasion) roaming naturally. There's a walking safari tour that's well worth your while, as you'll see all the best parts of the park, and your guide will know what to do if you have a close encounter of the scary kind. Incorporate a visit to Erzsébet lookout tower. This tiny castle-like building affords stunning views of Budapest, though the structure was damaged during Communism due to the giant red star that was crudely strapped to its zenith. From here, you can then get the chairlift back down to Buda.

Egyetemi Botanikus Kert (University Botanical Gardens)

Spread over 3 hectares (7 acres) of land, these peaceful gardens belong to the Eötvös Loránd University. An easy escape to where the palms sway and the children play, and perfect for a picnic. ⓐ VIII. Illés utca 25 Ⓣ (1) 314 0535 Ⓛ 09.00–17.00 Ⓜ Metro: Klinikák

▶ *Aquincum – Roman ruins in the Budapest suburbs*

Kozma utcai zsidó temető (Kozma Street Jewish Cemetery)

Opened in 1893, the city's main Jewish cemetery is a long tram ride from the centre of town. More than 500,000 people are buried here, many in vast and elaborate tombs that bear witness to the wealth and influence afforded the Budapest Jews before World War II. Here you will find Hungary's most moving Holocaust memorial: a set of nine walls with the names of victims etched into it. Only about 7,000 names appear, 1 per cent of the estimated 700,000 Hungarian Jews who perished in the war. Survivors and relatives continue to pencil in hundreds of additional names. The cemetery is still in use today.
ⓐ X. Kozma utca 6 🕐 08.00–16.00 Mon–Thur, 08.00–14.00 Fri & Sun, closed Sat Ⓜ Metro: Blaha Lujza tér, then tram 37

Margitsziget (Margaret Island)

This island oasis in the heart of Budapest is neither Buda nor Pest, but Margaret Island. Inhabited since Roman times, it was named after Princess Margaret, daughter of the 13th-century King Béla IV. Poor nine-year-old Margaret didn't get a chance to enjoy the splendour of her island, as King Béla made a pact with God that he would give her to a nunnery built on the island in return for some heavenly protection against the Mongols. The ruins of the convent are still visible today on the island's east bank. Since then, medieval kings have gambolled about, monks have gone about their quiet business and Budapesters from the 1860s onwards have made the island their playground. If you're not into the peace and tranquillity, you can visit a UNESCO-protected water tower, a musical fountain, an open-air stage, the Palatinus Strand swimming pool, two spa hotels or various restaurants and cafés that dot the island. Pedal cars can be hired

◀ *Margaret Island is a quiet, green oasis*

and picnicking is recommended. Ⓝ Metro: Nyugati pu, then bus 26 or tram 4 or 6

Pálvölgyi Cseppkő Barlang (Pálvölgyi Stalactite Cave)

This cave is known for its interesting stalactite formations that resemble animals (some say elephants, some say crocodiles; whatever you say, some interesting psychological profiling is sure to follow). Much of the cave is accessible by public steps, but some of the more interesting formations need to be seen with a guide. The air is supposed to have a curative medicinal effect – it is said to be especially good for hangovers. Remember to bring a sweater because the caves are cool. Admission is 1,000 HUF. Ⓐ II. Szépvölgyi út 162 Ⓣ (1) 325 9505 Ⓛ 10.00–16.00 Tues–Sun, closed Mon Ⓝ Bus: 65

Szemlő-hegyi Barlang (Szemlő Hill Cave)

The forlorn entrance to the cave doesn't hint at the marvels you'll see once inside. The remarkable formations of pisolite, which look like bunches of grapes, were formed in areas where thermal water permeated the limestone. Its cool, moist air has a curative effect for those suffering from respiratory problems or an underactive sex drive. Admission is 1,000 HUF. Ⓐ II. Pusztaszeri út 35 Ⓣ (1) 325 6001 Ⓛ 10.00–16.00 Wed–Mon, closed Tues Ⓝ Bus: 29

Szoborpark (Statue Park)

This park is either a kitsch gimmick or a commitment to remembering a harsh reality. While most of Eastern Europe resolutely destroyed all socialist statuary after the fall of the Communist regime in 1989, Hungarians decided to preserve this history, plucking most of the

◗ *A strident reminder of the Communist past?*

public art in Budapest and surrounding areas and depositing it here, thus creating a bizarre theme park in tribute to some terrible times. It's not surprising, as Hungarians want to remember more than they want to forget. There is one exception: you won't find any Stalin here. After the 1956 revolution, massive Stalin statues went missing. Back then, the various statues represented Soviet strength and unity. Today, out on the edge of town, and placed in almost comical positions, they've lost much of their dignity. The collection is a bit on the sparse side. It's definitely worth a look, but not as impressive as most guidebooks would have you believe. The gift-shop sells all sorts of Communist-era memorabilia, such as t-shirts, medals and cassettes of Red Army marching songs. ⓐ XXII. Balatoni út ⓣ (1) 424 7500 ⓦ www.szoborpark.hu ⓛ 10.00–dusk ⓝ Bus: 50. Admission charge

Vasúttörténeti Park (Railway History Park)

Remember the days you spent playing with a trainset as a child? Those were the days, and the Railway History Park is the place to pursue your childhood fantasy, and try your hand at being a conductor. There's plenty to gawk at: more than 100 old locomotives, including 50 vintage engines. Using a simulator modelled on the most powerful electric engine in Hungary, you can travel at 140 km (87 miles) per hour. Once you've practised, you'll have the chance to drive a real steam engine on a track 800 m (2,600 ft) long. If you get hungry with all the excitement, the Nostalgia Café serves light refreshments. From April to October, a vintage diesel shuttle train runs between Nyugati pu and the park. ⓐ XIV. Tatai út 95 ⓣ (1) 450 1497 ⓛ 10.00–15.00 Tues–Sun, 15–31 Mar; 10.00–18.00 Tues–Sun, 1 Apr–29 Oct; 10.00–15.00 Tues–Sun, 30 Oct–17 Dec, closed Mon & 18 Dec–14 Mar ⓝ Bus: 30; HÉV: 14

ⓞ *Wandering through the narrow streets of Eger*

OUT OF TOWN
trips

Szentendre

Szentendre, a mere 20 km (12 miles) north of the hustle and bustle of Budapest, is a perfect day trip for those interested in escaping the heat of the capital and dipping their toes into Hungarian culture. During their brief stay, the Romans named the town Ulcisia Castra (Wolf Camp), then packed up and left. In the late 16th and early 17th centuries, Serbs fled to this area while escaping Ottoman attack, and settled here permanently, building wooden houses of worship, then later reaching deeper into their pockets to make the baroque masterpieces we see today. Churches facing east on streets peppered with Serbian-style houses give Szentendre a distinctly Mediterranean feel.

Much of the Serbian population left in the 19th century, tired of fighting the flooding Danube and crop blight. As in so many small villages, disaster and lack of financial resources had a positive impact on preservation. The industrial revolution largely bypassed this cultural backwater by the Danube, leaving its lovely baroque buildings intact.

In the 1920s, Hungarian artists rediscovered Szentendre. This town of seven spires gave them an artistic imperative to set up their easels, and a popular artists' colony was born. Tourists soon got wind of the creative atmosphere, making this the popular destination it is today. In a town with a population of 20,000, it's rare to see ancient churches, historical and contemporary museums, small galleries, chic cafés, affordable restaurants and hotels, and tacky souvenir shops all comfortably sharing the same space. Grand baroque houses teeter on haphazardly built streets; unexpected alleyways lead just as often to a grandmother's kitchen as to an Orthodox church; and artists strive to capture

the mottled hues of yesteryear. The Orthodox churches still function, breathing the air of the past into a town that hasn't forgotten its origins.

GETTING THERE

By rail
A suburban train known as the HÉV will take you from Batthyány tér to Szentendre in just 45 minutes. Trains marked 'Szentendre' run every 20 minutes throughout the day, until 23.00. Buy your tickets at the station. For timetable information, call ☎ (1) 368 8814

By road
Volánbusz buses go from Árpád híd bus station to Szentendre with varying frequency between 06.30 and 22.40 each day. They arrive at bay 5 of Szentendre bus station, right next to the HÉV terminus. The journey takes 30 minutes. Buy your tickets on the bus. For timetable information, call ☎ (26) 382 0888 or see ⓦ www.volanbusz.hu

By water
This is the most recommended and romantic route, which follows the gently curving Danube from Budapest to Szentendre in a little over an hour-and-a-half. The boat leaves the Mahart quay at Vigadó tér each day at 10.30 and 14.30. A return boat leaves the quay at Szentendre at 17.00 and 19.00. Boats usually run until

---

▶ *Women working the fields in the bend of the Danube*

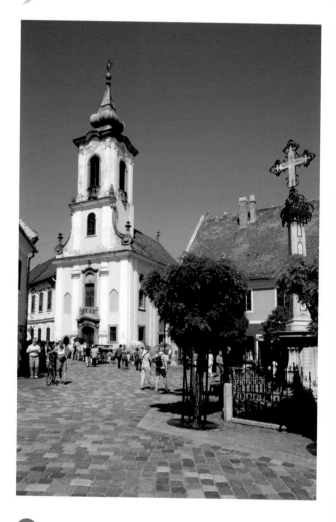

TOURIST INFORMATION

So many tourists, so many tourist information centres.
The following are the most helpful:

IBUSZ Gives you all the information you need to make the most of Szentendre. ⓐ Corner of Bogdányi út and Gőzhajó utca ⓣ (26) 310 181 ⓦ www.ibusz.hu ⓛ 09.00–17.00 Mon–Fri, 10.00–14.00 Sat & Sun, Apr–Oct; 09.00–16.00 Mon–Fri, closed Sat & Sun, Nov–Mar

Jági Utazás Has very friendly and knowledgeable staff, who will help you with your itinerary and make fair and impartial recommendations for the best eats and sleeps in town. ⓐ Kucsera Ferenc utca 15 ⓣ (26) 500 252 ⓛ 10.00–18.00 Mon–Fri, in season; 09.00–17.00 Mon–Fri, out of season; closed Sat & Sun

Tourinform Provides you with maps and an earful of information about concerts, exhibitions and accommodation. ⓐ Dumtsa Jenő utca 22 ⓣ (26) 317 965 ⓛ 09.00–19.00 Mon–Fri, 09.00–14.00 Sat & Sun, Apr–Oct; 09.00–17.00 Mon–Fri, closed Sat & Sun, Nov–Mar

mid-October. Buy your tickets at the quayside, with round trips from Vigadó tér to Szentendre costing 2,235 HUF. For timetable information, call ⓣ (1) 318 1223

◀ *Fő tér, the pretty town square in Szentendre*

SIGHTS & ATTRACTIONS

Szentendre is centred on Fő tér, its main square, with windy, cobbled streets radiating in all directions. Be assured that you will have no problem locating art galleries, souvenir shops or cafés, which seem to sprout from every crooked street corner. In the middle of Fő tér stands the Memorial Cross, which was erected by townsfolk in gratitude for being spared from the plague, another plus in living far removed from the big city.

Ámos Imre–Anna Margit Múzeum

Once an artist couple's home, this museum shows how opposites attract. Margit Anna's work is surprisingly accessible, harking back to children's paintings and folk themes. Imre Ámos's art is haunting, relating back to his Jewish heritage, and some of his best work was done between periods of forced labour on the Russian front. His last work predicts his own demise; he died of typhus. ⓐ Bogdányi utca 12 ⓣ (26) 310 790 ⓛ 10.00–18.00 (summer); 13.00–17.00 (winter). Admission charge

Barcsay Múzeum

Jenő Barcsay (1900–88) represents Hungarian 20th-century art as a proponent of constructivism, an art movement of the 1920s that rejected 'pure' art forms and favoured socialist art. Through his public-building mosaics and wall textiles, we can see his creative genius at its best. The *Madman of the Village*, *Working Girl* and *Working Woman* are excellent examples of how he escaped the restrictions of socialism through expressionism. ⓐ Dumtsa Jenő utca 10 ⓣ (26) 310 244 ⓛ 10.00–18.00 Tues–Sun, closed Mon. Admission charge

Blagovestenska Templom (Blagovestenska Church)

If you get the feeling someone's watching you, that's because all the icons are looking at you. This use of iconography was the most effective way to get the illiterate masses to pay attention during services. The Rococo windows facing out on to Görög utca will also catch your eye. This Serbian Orthodox church was built in the mid-18th century. ❸ Fő tér 4 🕓 10.00–17.00 Tues–Sun, closed Mon

Czóbel Béla Múzeum

This museum is housed in what was once a Catholic school on Szentendre's Castle Hill. Béla Czóbel (1883–1976) lived and worked from 1940 to 1966 in Szentendre, and from 1966 to 1967 in Budapest. The selection of portraits, still lifes and landscapes are from these periods. Information about the artist and works is in English. He's so popular that some of his art was lifted from the Museum of Fine Arts in Budapest (see page 94). ❸ Templom tér 1 ☎ (26) 312 721 🕓 10.00–18.00 Tues–Sun, closed Mon. Admission charge

Ferenczy Károly Múzeum

This museum contains historical, archaeological and ethnographic collections, as well as paintings, and is dedicated to the art of the extraordinary Ferenczy family, particularly the patriarch Károly Ferenczy, one of Hungary's most famous Impressionists. Works by Ferenczy's children, who were excellent artists in their own right, are also on display. ❸ Fő tér 6 ☎ (26) 310 244 🕓 10.00–18.00 Wed–Sun (summer); 10.00–16.00 Wed–Sun (winter), closed Mon & Tues. Admission charge

Kovács Margit Múzeum

Margit Kovács (1907–77) is a celebrated potter in Hungary. The museum limits entry to 20 people at a time, so try to visit either early in the morning or at lunchtime. ⓐ Vastagh György utca 1 ⓣ (26) 310 244 ⓞ 10.00–18.00 Tues–Sun, Apr–Oct; 10.00–16.00 Tues–Sun, Nov–Mar, closed Mon

Pap Sziget (Priest's Island)

If you bring swimming gear to Szentendre, you can take a bus to this little island at the northern end of town, which boasts thermal waters in outdoor bathing pools. There is no admission, and there are some lockers to stash your cash, as well as towel hire. It's a

20-minute walk, or take the bus for Leányfalu and Visegrád; when you pass the bridge, get out at Pap Sziget.

Skanzen

This open-air museum is 3 km (2 miles) from Szentendre. It's a living museum that faithfully depicts village life in Hungary from the end of the 18th century to the beginning of the 20th century. The villagers living under the thatched roofs of the village show visitors how to weave, cook, smith and work wood with all the historical tools of the trade. A market replete with farm animals milling about makes this a perfect excursion if you have children.

Skanzen re-creates Hungarian village life

ANOTHER MUSEUM, ANYONE?

If you're into twee museums, try the **Szabó Marzipan Museum** (🄰 Dumtsa Jenő utca 14), which serves a marzipan version of Michael Jackson, or the **Dobos Confectionery Museum** (🄰 Nosztalgia Ház, Bogdányi utca 2), where you can get some real Dobostorta (chocolate cake with a hard caramel topping). Or what about the **House of Folk Arts** (🄰 Rákóczi utca 1) or the **Roman Stone Collection** (🄰 Dunakanyari Boulevard 1), where you'll find ancient artefacts from the Roman town of Ulcisia Castra? The **Art Mill** (🄰 Bogdányi utca 32) is a living workshop of contemporary arts with exhibitions. The **Baby Museum** (🄰 Sas utca 18) is fun for children, as is the **National Wine Museum** (🄰 Bogdányi utca 10) for harried parents and wine lovers.

To get there, take the bus from bay 7 of Szentendre's bus station. By car, follow route 11, and turn left at Sztaravodai utca. A family ticket is available, as well as English-language information about the museum. 🄣 (26) 502 500 🄦 www.skanzen.hu 🄛 09.00–17.00 Tues–Sun, closed Mon, Apr–Oct; 10.00–15.00 Sat–Sun, closed weekdays, Nov; closed Dec–Mar. Admission charge

Szerb Ortodox Múzeum (Serbian Orthodox Museum)

This museum has a collection of icons from the 16th to 19th centuries, liturgical vessels and Ottoman-period scrolls in Arabic.

🄳 *The peaceful garden of the Serbian Orthodox Museum*

Information is in English. ⓐ Pátriárka utca 5 ⓣ (26) 312 399
ⓛ 10.00–17.00 Tues–Sun, closed Mon, Apr–Oct; 10.00–16.00
Fri–Sun, closed Mon–Thur, Nov–Mar. Admission charge

TAKING A BREAK

Cafés, restaurants and pubs spill out on to the pavements in the
summer, giving the streets of Szentendre that European, lived-in
look. With so many places to choose from, you will be hard-pressed
to stay hungry. Most are concentrated around Fő tér and along the
river. If you're interested in checking out the local music scene,
there are a few music clubs in town.

Kedvenc Kifőzde £ ❶ A small lunch spot that serves some of
the best quick meals in town. ⓐ Bükkös part 21 ⓣ (26) 319 186
ⓛ 12.00–16.00 Mon–Fri, 12.00–15.00 Sat, closed Sun

Mar Mediterraneo £ ❷ Warm and friendly, serving light salads
and other dishes with a Mediterranean flair. ⓐ Pannónia utca 8
ⓣ (26) 314 185 ⓛ 12.00–22.00

Rab Ráby £ ❸ A favourite with the locals, specialising in fish.
ⓐ Kucsera F utca 1/a ⓣ (26) 310 819 ⓛ 12.00–22.00 Tues–Sun,
closed Mon

Sandros Étterem ££ ❹ Romantic, classy Hungarian with wrought-
iron balustrades and comfortable seating. Perfect for a first date.
ⓐ Dézsma utca 2 ⓛ 12.00–22.00 Tues–Sun, closed Mon

ACCOMMODATION

HOTELS & GUESTHOUSES

Centrum Panzió £ Big rooms, some with river views, and staff catering to your every need: massages, a play area for children with toys and a filling breakfast. ⓐ Duna korzó, on the river north of Fő tér

Corner Panzió £ Set in a historical house, the rooms have been converted tastefully, with lots of blond wood and simple IKEA-like furnishings. A quiet family hotel in the heart of town. ⓐ Duna korzó 4 ⓣ (26) 301 524

Hotel Róz £ A friendly guesthouse with a small garden overlooking the Danube for breakfast when weather permits. All rooms have 3-star amenities, and the hotel has its own restaurant serving fish, chicken and, of course, goulash. ⓐ Pannónia utca 6/b ⓣ (26) 311 737 ⓦ www.hotelrozszentendre.hu

Mathias Rex Panzió £–££ A wide range of rooms in this bed and breakfast, which also has a garden, secure parking, good breakfasts and a non-smoking floor. ⓐ Kossuth utca 16 ⓣ (26) 50 55 70 ⓕ (26) 50 55 73 ⓔ info@mathiasrexhotel.hu

CAMPSITE

Pap Sziget (Priest's Island) Pap has a campsite at 3,500 HUF for a tent. ⓣ (26) 31 06 97 ⓔ info@pap-sziget.hu ⓛ Apr–Oct, closed Nov–Mar

Eger

A minaret stands sentinel in this proud country town, 126 km (78 miles) northeast of Budapest, demarcating the furthest northern expansion in Europe of the Ottoman Turks. The siege of Eger lasted for over a month in 1552, when fewer than 2,500 soldiers and women repelled Turkish forces, who outnumbered them by 40 to 1, with whatever they could find – rocks, soup, hot fat, you name it. A proud moment in Hungarian history, the theme of 'The women defenders of Eger' is reflected in numerous paintings, poems and monuments throughout the country. Descendants of the famous women of Eger still meet today, but their activities in defence of the town are purely peaceful.

It's a town well worth defending. As Hungary's third most popular tourist destination, Eger offers an affordable taste of Hungary's history and cuisine, offering the truly Magyar experience for those who are interested. Its combination of soaring architectural sights, cosy wine cellars, a small-town feel and bustling, market-square activity is sure to please. The blend of old and new creates a lively atmosphere: upmarket shops, wine bars and restaurants, along with the ancient ruins of Eger Castle and the Turkish minaret, compete for your attention.

This historical wine area has been producing wines since the 11th century. Its best-known wine is Egri Bikavér, also known as Bull's Blood, forever linked with the strength and courage of Hungary's resistance to foreign powers. Don't leave Eger without testing some of the wonderful varieties in the nearby Szépasszony-völgy (Valley of Beautiful Women, see page 138), in the many old wine cellars dug into the hillside. The mould on many of the wine-cellar walls is so thick that you can stick a coin on it to commemorate your visit.

There are quite a few festivals and events happening in Eger during the summer, the cream of the crop being the Bull's Blood wine competition in July, and Eger Baroque Days from the end of July to mid-August, a splendiferous mix of classical concerts, dancing, laser light shows, theatre performances and cinema. Go to ⓦ www.egeronline.com for more information about events.

GETTING THERE

By rail

From Budapest's Keleti Station, there are 34 trains leaving for Eger daily; the journey takes about two hours. The railway station in Eger is on Állomás tér, about one km (half a mile) from the town centre. Depending on the time of day you travel, the full fare for a second-class ticket ranges from 2,290 HUF to 3,440 HUF.

By road

Take the M3 motorway in the direction of Miskolc, then exit at Füzesabony and follow the signs to Eger. There are a few car parks in town and you can buy your parking ticket at the coin-operated machines nearby. The historical town centre is only open to pedestrians and drivers with permits.

SIGHTS & ATTRACTIONS

All of Eger's historical sites are within easy walking distance if you start at Dobó István tér, the main square of town. The Minorite Church, a fine 18th-century baroque gem, is worth a look. Two

● *There's a great view of the town from the castle ramparts*

TOURIST INFORMATION

For information, or securing accommodation, visit **Tourinform** (❷ Dobó István tér 2 ☎ (36) 517 715 ⏰ 09.00–18.00 Mon–Fri, 10.00–13.00 Sat & Sun, in season; 10.00–13.00 Mon–Sat, closed Sun out of season). Private rooms can be booked at **Egertourist** (❸ Bajcsy-Zsilinszky utca 9 ☎ (36) 411 225 ⏰ 10.00–18.00 Mon–Sat, closed Sun).

statues dominate the square: one of István Dobó, town defender during the great siege, and the other of Magyars fighting against the Turks.

The famous Eger Castle is a prominent stronghold visible from just about anywhere in town. You can wander the grounds free of charge, or visit the two museums that make their homes there. The István Dobó Castle Museum is choc-a-bloc with Turkish artefacts, and gives you the general history of the castle. **Eger Picture Gallery** has a fine collection of Hungarian artists (⏰ 10.00–17.00 Tues–Sun (summer); 10.00–16.00 Tues–Sun (winter), closed Mon. Admission charge).

Just to the west of the castle, on Harangöntő utca, is Eger's imposing minaret, a visible reminder of the Turkish presence in the area. Though the town valiantly fought against the Ottoman Empire in 1552, it only stalled it for a few years. In 1596, Sultan Mohammed III was able to capture the castle, and the Turks ruled Eger until 1687, building mosques and baths. After the Turks retreated, there were only 3,500 residents in the town, including 600 Muslims who

◀ *The István Dobó Castle Museum is one of the most popular in Hungary* converted to Christianity and assimilated into Hungarian life. The minaret, which is 35 m (115 ft) tall, survives to this day in remarkably good condition, although the mosque that it belonged to was destroyed. For a small fee, you can ascend its cramped and dizzying spiral staircase and be rewarded with a spectacular view of the town below. Buy tickets for the minaret at its base (🕐 10.00–18.00 (summer); 10.00–16.00 (winter)).

South of the minaret on Eszterházy tér is the second-largest church in Hungary, Eger's **Basilica** (🕐 06.00–19.00). This neoclassical building was built in the 1830s, replacing a medieval church that stood on the same spot. If you catch it in time to hear an organ recital in the summer, you'll bear witness to its awesome acoustics.

Opposite the basilica is the **Károly Eszterházy Lyceum** (🕐 09.30–15.00 Tues–Sun, closed Mon (summer); 09.30–13.00 Sat & Sun, closed Mon–Fri (winter)), Eger's finest example of 18th-century architecture. It's worth climbing up to the 11th storey and gazing out from the observatory at the top. Have a look at the frescoes that decorate the ceiling of the library. The latter contains the first Hungarian printed book, dating from 1473. Outdoor performances are frequently scheduled in the summer months.

Eger's **Turkish Baths** (🅰 Fürdő utca 1–3 🕐 14.00–18.00 Sat, 08.00–18.00 Sun, closed Mon–Fri) were built at the beginning of the 17th century, and are perfect to soothe your tired travel muscles. They're mixed-sex, with spa services posted in English.

The former home of Serbian fairy-tale author Mihály Vitkovics (🅰 Széchenyi István út 🕐 (36) 412 023) is worth a visit for an insight into local 18th-century literature.

▶ *The Basilica in Eger is Hungary's second-largest church*

TAKING A BREAK

There are cake shops and snack stands all around town where you can fuel up satisfyingly and cheaply. There aren't really any international eateries in this town, unless you consider pizza international. Here, it doesn't really matter where you go: you'll be served a surprisingly large platter of Hungarian specialities, described on the menu with choice phrases like 'The pleasures of the women of Eger', 'Foot of peasant' and 'Cow steps on István Dobó Square'.

Dobos Cukrászda £ ❶ A conveniently located little restaurant and coffee house that serves strong coffee and breakfast early, before the summer heat sets in, on Dobó István tér. ⓐ Széchenyi István utca 6 ❶ (36) 413 335 ⏱ 09.30–19.30

Fehér Szarvas Vadásztanya £ ❷ A hunting inn, conveniently located south of Dobó István tér, which offers a full range of Hungarian wild-game specialities complemented by some good Hungarian vintage. More restaurant than café, this is popular with locals and tourists alike, so make a reservation if you can. ⓐ Klapka György utca 8 ❶ (36) 411 129 ⏱ 12.00–00.00

Szenátor Ház £ ❸ Locals seem to flock to this place. Eger is one of the few places in Hungary that serves strong Turkish coffee, a great way to start the morning, especially when coupled with a *túró süti*, a Hungarian pastry filled with curd cheese and raisins. ⓐ Dobó István tér 11 ❶ (36) 320 466 ⏱ 11.00–22.00

◀ *Eger's restaurants serve hearty Hungarian food*

VALLEY OF BEAUTIFUL WOMEN

If you take a 30-minute walk southwest from town, or a quick taxi ride, you will end up at the Szépasszony-völgy (Valley of Beautiful Women). Carved into the hillside, more than 200 wine cellars offer their own special vintage. If you're lucky, you'll go to a wine cellar that serves up live music with the wine; it can get quite lively after a few. Grab a quick snack from the stands serving nuts and crisps around the wine cellars, or a meal from one of the restaurants in the nearby village – good for cleansing your palate before the next tasting. The cellars open at noon and close early, most around 22.00.

ACCOMMODATION

HOTELS & GUESTHOUSES

Garten Vendéghaz £ A welcome respite for those wanting to get away from it all. The views from this guesthouse located in the hills overlooking Eger are beautiful, but even nicer is the price you pay for such a pretty spot. ❷ Legányi utca 6 ❶ (36) 420 371

Bacchus Panzió £–££ This tidy little bed and breakfast serves up lots of charm. Perfect after a bit too much Bull's Blood. The rooms are nicely furnished, and there's a garden at the back. ❸ Szépasszony-völgy utca 29 ❶ (36) 428 950 ❼ www.bacchuspanzio.hu ❺ bacchuspanzio@axelero.hu

❶ *Wine cellars are carved into the hillside just outside the town*

Hotel Korona ££ Clean and cosy on a quiet residential street near Dobó István tér. Breakfast and wellness-sauna, whirlpool and swimming pool served up in style. There's even a 200-year-old wine cellar on the property, where you can taste some of Eger's finest. ⓐ Tündérpart 5 ⓣ (36) 310 287 ⓦ www.koronahotel.hu

Hotel Minaret ££ Next to the minaret, this hotel offers simple and tidy digs with breakfast. Great price for the location, and friendly management. ⓐ Knézich K utca 4 ⓣ (36) 410 233 ⓦ www.hotelminaret.hu

Hotel Romantik ££ This family-oriented 3-star is located in the centre of Eger, about 50 m (160 ft) from Széchenyi utca, Eger's main pedestrian street. ⓐ Csíky S utca 26 ⓣ (36) 310 456

Szenátor Ház ££ Sitting right on Dobó István tér, the location and price can't be beaten, neither can the atmosphere of this small, friendly hotel. ⓐ Dobó István tér 11 ⓣ (36) 320 466

CAMPSITES
Tulipán Kemping The campsite is within stumbling distance of the Szépasszony-völgy wine cellars and charges 500 HUF per tent, 600 HUF per person, 300 HUF tourism tax, 300 HUF per car. The site has shower and restaurant facilities, and cabins to rent out for very reasonable rates. The proprietors also own the affordable **Hotel Rubinia**, located next to the site. ⓐ Szépasszony-völgy 71 ⓣ (36) 410 580 ⓔ info@hotelrubinia.hu ⓒ Apr–Oct, closed Nov–Mar

---

◑ *Tramlines run along the Danube*

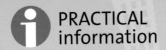

Directory

GETTING THERE

By air

easyJet (ⓦ www.easyjet.com), **Jet2.com** (ⓦ www.jet2.com), **Wizz Air** (ⓦ www.wizzair.com), **BA** (ⓦ www.britishairways.com) and **Lufthansa** (ⓦ www.lufthansa.com) all fly to Budapest's Ferihegy Airport (see page 48), which is 24 km (15 miles) southeast of the city centre. It has three terminals: Terminal 1, which serves a small number of budget airlines; Terminal 2A, which serves Malév Hungarian Airlines; and the busy Terminal 2B, which serves most of the international and budget airlines and welcomes around four million passengers. For general information about the airport, call ⓘ (1) 296 9696; for flight information, call ⓘ (1) 296 5959 or visit ⓦ www.bud.hu. The journey time from UK airports is approximately two-and-a-quarter hours.

From North America, Alitalia and British Airways both fly routes into Budapest, with the flight time around nine hours from New York and 12 hours from Atlanta. Virgin Atlantic flies into Budapest, with a stopover in the UK and the journey time's around 27 hours. If you're flying from New Zealand, you can book flights with BA or **Qantas** (ⓦ www.qantas.com.au) but again there are stopovers (the US/UK and Australia/Thailand respectively), with the journey time around 29 hours. That's a lot of in-flight movies to watch...

Many people are aware that air travel emits CO_2, which contributes to climate change. You may be interested in the possibility of lessening the environmental impact of your flight through the charity Climate Care, which offsets your CO_2 by funding environmental projects around the world. Visit ⓦ www.climatecare.org

🔺 *The Tisza Express to Moscow waits at Keleti Station*

By rail

More than 50 trains a day provide direct links between Budapest and no fewer than 25 other capital cities. Trains from Vienna to Budapest run regularly, and the journey takes about three-and-a-half hours. For planning a longer train journey to Budapest, consult the monthly **Thomas Cook European Rail Timetable**, which has up-to-date schedules for European international and national train services (Ⓦ www.thomascookpublishing.com).

By road

International coach services run to and from **Népliget** coach station
(ⓐ IX. Üllői út 131 ⓣ (1) 219 8080 ⓛ 06.00–20.00). For planning a
coach journey to Budapest, contact **Eurolines** (ⓦ www.eurolines.co.uk).

If you choose to drive yourself, be aware that speed limits
are 130 kph (80 mph) on motorways, 110 kph (68 mph) on dual
carriageways, 90 kph (56 mph) on other roads and 50 kph
(31 mph) in built-up areas. It is compulsory to wear seatbelts in
both front and back seats and prohibited to use mobile phones
when the car is in motion. There is zero tolerance of drink-driving
in Hungary.

The M1, M3, M5 and M7 are toll motorways that will link you
to Budapest from all directions and you must pay the appropriate
toll either at the border or at larger petrol stations. Make sure you
display the sticker in your windscreen.

The border crossings from Austria and Slovakia are hassle-free.
Hungary no longer requires the international driving permit. Cars
entering Hungary are required to have a sticker indicating the
country of registration, a first-aid kit and an emergency triangle.

The Hungarian Automobile Club (ⓐ II. Rómer Flóris utca 4/a
ⓣ (1) 345 1800) offers 24-hour roadside assistance and emergency
roadside help (ⓣ 188 in a crisis).

By water

A hydrofoil service along the Danube runs from 1 May to 29 October.
The journey to Budapest takes six-and-a-half hours from Vienna
(22,735 HUF) and four-and-a-half hours from Bratislava (20,180 HUF).
You will arrive at Belgrad rakpart. The service is operated by **Mahart
PassNave Ltd** (ⓣ (1) 484 4010 ⓦ www.mahartpassnave.hu
ⓔ hydrofoil@mahartpassnave.hu).

ENTRY FORMALITIES

Citizens of the UK, the Republic of Ireland, the US, Canada, Australia and New Zealand need only a valid passport to enter Hungary for up to 90 days. Citizens of other countries should contact the nearest Hungarian embassy for details of visa requirements.

Visitors to Hungary from within the EU are entitled to bring their personal effects and goods for personal consumption and not for resale, which can be up to 800 cigarettes and 10 litres of spirits. Those entering the country from outside the EU may bring 200 cigarettes (50 cigars, 250 g tobacco), 2 litres of wine and 1 litre of spirits. No meat or milk products are permitted to be brought into the country from inside or outside the EU.

MONEY

The Hungarian currency is the *forint* (HUF). Coins in circulation are 1, 2, 5, 10, 20, 50 and 100 HUF. Banknotes come in denominations of 200, 500, 1,000, 2,000, 5,000, 10,000 and 20,000 HUF. You can use your credit card in tourist-related businesses such as hotels, restaurants, petrol stations and the more central shops, but often not in museums, supermarkets and train or bus stations. For this reason, it's a good idea always to have some cash on you. ATMs are on just about every street corner and are the place to go for a quick top-up of finances. Euros, US dollars and British pounds are acceptable forms of payment at higher-end accommodation facilities.

If you want to change some money, there are convenient 24-hour exchange machines that offer good bank rates. You can find them in many places, such as Margit körút 43–45, Károly körút 20, Váci utca 40, Andrássy út 49 and elsewhere. Don't use Interchange or the exchange kiosks around Váci utca: they're a misleading rip-off, as they post good rates that apply only if you change a lot of money. Don't even

● *Police zip through the smaller streets of Budapest in their Smart cars*

think about changing money on the black market; it's illegal, and you get better rates at the 24-hour exchange machines anyway.

HEALTH, SAFETY & CRIME

No jabs or inoculations are required for entry to Hungary. To be on the safe side, bring enough of any prescription or other medication you may need. Always pack a copy of all prescriptions in case you run out of any medication. You can find sunscreen and other toiletries, in addition to over-the-counter medications, at any chemist. The biggest complaint among travellers is an upset stomach, probably brought on by mixing paprika and alcohol.

Air pollution in Budapest, though bad, is getting better, as a ring road now redirects long-distance lorries around the city. The water is perfectly safe to drink. Smoking is prohibited in all public places, including on public transport. Unfortunately for non-smokers, smoking is still publicly accepted in restaurants and pubs, so expect your lungs to get a little black in exchange for some ambience.

Budapest is generally a safe city, and violent street crime is practically non-existent. Boisterous drunks are a nuisance, but almost never pose a serious threat. That said, you should always be on the lookout for pickpockets, especially on crowded buses, trains and trams. Pickpockets generally work in teams, with one or more creating a distraction (bumping into people, falling down, staging a fake argument and so on), while a partner takes advantage. One way to protect yourself is by always carrying valuables in an inside pocket or in a money belt.

Be wary of overly friendly women, particularly on touristy thoroughfares. The *konzum lány*, or 'consumption girl', is an attractive young woman who approaches a foreigner, strikes up a conversation and then brings him to a bar she 'just happens to know'. After she gets him to buy her a drink, the foreigner is presented with an outlandish bill. A few brutes materialise out of nowhere and make the foreigner pay, and the girl goes back out on the street, ready for her next victim.

To register a complaint about a scam of any kind, contact the **Fogyasztóvédelmi Főfelügyelőség**, or **Bureau of Consumer Affairs** (ⓐ VIII. József körút 6 ❶ (1) 459 4800 or 459 4945 ⓛ 08.00–18.00 Mon–Thur, 09.00–14.00 Fri, closed Sat & Sun).

OPENING HOURS

Banks 🕐 08.00–15.00 Mon–Thur, 08.00–13.00 Fri
Clothes shops 🕐 10.00–18.00 Mon–Sat
Food shops 🕐 07.00–18.00 Mon–Sat
Offices 🕐 08.00–16.00 Mon–Fri
Post Offices 🕐 08.00–16.00 Mon–Fri, 08.00–13.00 Sat

TOILETS

Few public toilets exist in Buda or Pest, so locals and tourists use the toilets in cafés and restaurants. You just have to pay the attendant after using the facilities. Toilets in shopping centres also provide quick relief.

Toilets in bars and wine or beer cellars are often free. Note also that while Budapest's main railway stations have public toilets, most metro stations do not.

Toilets signposted in Hungarian usually have the words *Nők* or *Női* (women) and *Férfiak* or *Férfi* (men). Occasionally, signs for *Hölgyek* (ladies) and *Urak* (gentlemen) also appear.

CHILDREN

You and your children will have an absolute blast in Budapest. The three main areas to go are the Buda Hills (see page 106), Margaret Island (see page 109) and the Városliget, or City Park (see page 93).

In the Buda Hills, you can go for long or short hikes, taking advantage of the fun modes of transport, such as a chairlift and special railways. On Margaret Island, the playground for adults and children in Budapest, you can hire a pedal car; visit a musical fountain, an old ruin and a small zoo (ⓐ XIV. Városliget, Állatkerti körút 6–12 ☎ (1) 363 3710), where children can pet some of the animals; or go splashing in the **Palatinus Strand** (ⓐ XIII. Margitsziget

🕐 (1) 340 4505), a fantastic outdoor swimming pool, or Hajós Alfréd pool for more serious swimmers. In the Városliget, you can visit the **Fun Fair** (Ⓐ XIV. Városliget, Állatkerti körút 14–16) or the **Capital Circus** (Ⓐ XIV. Városliget, Állatkerti körút 7 🕐 (1) 343 8300).

Elsewhere in the city, older children might enjoy the **Görzenál Skate and Leisure Park** (Ⓐ III. Árpád fejedelem út 2000 🕐 (1) 250 4800).

🔺 Take the kids along to the zoo for a great day out

Meanwhile, the **Laser Theatre Planetarium** (Ⓐ X. Népliget ☎ (1) 263 0871 🌐 www.lasertheatre.hu) has musical programmes and educational shows for different age groups. Science buffs will appreciate the **Palace of Wonders** (Ⓐ II. Fény u. 20-22 ☎ (1) 336 4000), where they can get hands-on with science experiments. Buda Castle Labyrinth (see page 67) is great for entertaining kids of all ages.

COMMUNICATIONS
Internet
In Budapest, there's internet access at just about every turn. Major hotels and shopping centres offer internet facilities as well. To find wireless hotspots in Budapest, go to 🌐 www.hotspotter.hu. The following is a list of conveniently located internet cafés:

AMI Ⓐ V. Váci utca 40 ☎ (1) 267 1644 🕐 09.00–00.00

ChatMan Internet Café Ⓐ VII. Dohány u. 30 ☎ (1) 266 0856 🕐 08.00–00.00 Mon–Fri, 10.00–00.00 Sat & Sun

Private Link Ⓐ VIII. József körút 52 ☎ (1) 334 2057 🕐 24 hrs

X-tra Net Ⓐ VIII. József körút 52-56 ☎ (1) 313 0893 🕐 24 hrs

Yellow Zebra Internet Café Ⓐ V. Sütő utca 2 ☎ (1) 226 8777 🕐 09.00–20.00

Phone
Hungary's modernised communications provider is Magyar Telekom. The quality of both landline and mobile services is good, with mobile services provided by T-Mobile, Vodafone and Pannon GSM.

For payphones, buy a phonecard at post offices, MOL petrol stations, travel agencies, Tesco supermarkets, newspaper kiosks, railway stations and T-Pont shops, for values of 800 HUF upwards. Coins (10, 20, 50 and 100 HUF) can also be used.

For directory enquiries, dial ☎ 198

TELEPHONING HUNGARY

To telephone Hungary from abroad, dial the international access code (00), followed by the country code (36), the appropriate area code (1 for Budapest, 36 for Eger, 26 for Szentendre) and the six- or seven-digit telephone number.

To make a long-distance call within Hungary, such as from Budapest to Szentendre, dial 06, followed by the area code (26) and the six-digit telephone number.

TELEPHONING ABROAD

To telephone home from Hungary, dial the international access code (00), followed by the appropriate country code (61 for Australia, 1 for Canada or the US, 64 for New Zealand, 353 for the Republic of Ireland, 44 for the UK), the area code (minus the initial 0, in the case of the UK) and the number you require.

Post

You can find square red post boxes with the post horn and envelope symbols throughout Budapest. Postage stamps are widely available at tobacconists.

The **Magyar Posta main post office** is at ⓐ V. Városház utca 18 ⓘ (1) 485 9011 ⓛ 08.00–20.00 Mon–Fri, 08.00–14.00 Sat, closed Sun ⓜ Metro: Deák tér

There are also post offices near Keleti and Nyugati railway stations. The post office near Keleti is at ⓐ VIII. Baross tér 11/c ⓘ (1) 322 9013 ⓛ 07.00–21.00 Mon–Fri, 08.00–14.00 Sat, closed Sun. The post office near Nyugati is at ⓐ VI. Teréz körút 51–53 ⓘ (1) 353 0860 ⓛ 08.00–20.00 Mon–Fri, 08.00–14.00 Sat, closed Sun

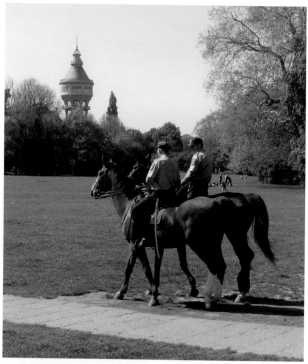

◓ *Mounted police on Margaret Island*

ELECTRICITY

The electrical current is supplied at 220 volts. Standard continental two-pin plugs are used, so an adaptor will be required for British and non-continental appliances. Americans and Canadians with 110-volt appliances will also need a voltage transformer.

TRAVELLERS WITH DISABILITIES

Many Budapest buildings are inaccessible to disabled travellers, and public transport can be difficult. The good news is that EU norms have influenced policy, making Hungary's museums, newer buildings and some public transport accessible. Gellért Baths (see page 67), for instance, were renovated in 2007 to improve access. The yellow metro line has a special motorised chair at the Deák tér, Mexikói út and Széchenyi fürdő stops. For information about disabled access while in Hungary, contact the **Hungarian Disabled Association (MEOSZ)** (ⓐ III. San Marco utca 76 ❶ (1) 388 5529 or 388 2387 ✉ meosz@meoszinfo.hu).

TOURIST INFORMATION

Tourinform is your best bet, with offices at the following locations:

Tourinform Belváros ⓐ V. Sütő utca 2 ❶ (1) 438 8080
🕐 08.00–20.00

Tourinform Buda Castle ⓐ I. Szentháromság tér ❶ (1) 488 0475
🕐 09.00–20.00

Tourinform Oktogon ⓐ VI. Liszt Ferenc tér 11 ❶ (1) 322 4098
🕐 10.00–18.00 Mon–Fri, 10.00–16.00 Sat & Sun

BACKGROUND READING

Culture Shock! Hungary by Zsuzsanna Ardó. Offers an unflinching but affectionate insight into the character of a nation.
Living in Hungary by Jean-Luc Soulé and Alain Fleischer. Couples world-class photography with inspirational travel ideas, to make an up-close-and-personal guide to the Hungarian way of living.
The Hungarians: A Thousand Years of Victory in Defeat by Paul Lendvai. An accessible, in-depth history of a proud, passionate people.

Emergencies

The following are emergency numbers:

Ambulance ☎ 104

Doctor ☎ (1) 200 0100

Fire ☎ 105

Police ☎ 107

Report a crime (in English) ☎ (1) 438 8080 or 06 80 555 111

MEDICAL SERVICES

For EU citizens, emergency medical treatment is provided free of charge in Hungary. The following are centrally located emergency chemists:

Mária ⓐ XIII. Béke tér 11 ☎ (1) 320 8006

Óbuda ⓐ II. Vörösvári út 84 ☎ (1) 368 6430

The following are surgeries with English-speaking doctors:

Belgyógyászati Klinika ⓐ VIII. Korányi Sándor utca 2/a ☎ (1) 210 0278
🕐 By appointment Mon–Fri

Dr Rose Medical Center ⓐ V. Roosevelt tér 7–8 ☎ (1) 377 6737
(non-stop hotline) 🕐 08.00–20.00 Mon–Fri, closed Sat & Sun

FirstMed Centers ⓐ I. Hattyú utca 14, 5th floor ☎ (1) 224 9090
🌐 www.firstmedcenters.com ✉ info@firstmedcenters.com 🕐 24 hrs

Rózsakert Medical Centre ⓐ II. Gábor Áron utca 74–78/a, 2nd floor
☎ (1) 391 5903 🕐 24 hrs

The following are surgeries with English-speaking dentists:

Fogorvosi Rendelő Dent–Ász Kft. ⓐ V. Károly körút 18 ☎ (1) 266 4906

SOS Dent ⓐ VI. Király utca 14 ☎ (1) 269 6010 🕐 24 hrs

Szent Rókus Kórház és Intézményei ⓐ VIII. Gyulai Pál utca 2
☎ (1) 266 8000

POLICE

If you are robbed, it's best to report it to the crime hotline (☎ (1) 438 8080, 06 80 201 303 or 107). If you need to fill in any forms, go to the **Central Police Station** (🏢 XIII. Teve Utca 4–6 ☎ (1) 443 5500 Ⓜ Metro: Arpád híd).

EMBASSIES & CONSULATES

Australia 🏢 XII. Királyhágó tér 8–9 ☎ (1) 457 9777 📠 201 9792
🌐 www.ausembbp.hu
Canada 🏢 II. Ganz utca 12–14 ☎ (1) 392 3360 🌐 www.dfait-maeci.gc.ca/budapest
New Zealand does not have an embassy in Budapest, but the British embassy can handle matters for New Zealand citizens or you can contact the honorary consulate ☎ (1) 302 2484
South Africa 🏢 II. Gárdonyi Géza utca 17 ☎ (1) 392 0999
✉️ saemb@sa-embassy.hu
UK 🏢 V. Harmincad utca 6 ☎ (1) 266 2888 🌐 www.britishembassy.hu
US 🏢 V. Szabadság tér 12 ☎ (1) 475 4400 🌐 www.usembassy.hu

EMERGENCY PHRASES

Help!	**Fire!**	**Stop!**
Segítség!	Tűz!	Állj!
Sheh-geet-shayg!	*Teewz!*	*Ahlly!*

Call an ambulance/a doctor/the police/the fire brigade!
Hivja a mentőket/orvost/rendőrséget/tűzoltókat!
Heev-yo o mehn-tur-keht/ohr-vohsht/rehn-dur-shay-geht/teewz-ohl-tooh-kot!

WHAT'S IN YOUR GUIDEBOOK?

Independent authors Impartial up-to-date information from our travel experts who meticulously source local knowledge.

Experience Thomas Cook's 165 years in the travel industry and guidebook publishing enriches every word with expertise you can trust.

Travel know-how Contributions by thousands of staff around the globe, each one living and breathing travel.

Editors Travel-publishing professionals, pulling everything together to craft a perfect blend of words, pictures, maps and design.

You, the traveller We deliver a practical, no-nonsense approach to information, geared to how you really use it.

Editorial/project management: Lisa Plumridge
Copy editor: Paul Hines
Layout/DTP: Pat Hinsley & Alison Rayner
Proofreader: Wendy Janes

SPOTTED YOUR NEXT CITY BREAK?

...then these lightweight CitySpots pocket guides will have you in the know in no time, wherever you're heading. Covering over 80 cities worldwide, they're packed with detail on the most important urban attractions from shopping and sights to non-stop nightlife; knocking spots off chunkier, clunkier versions.

Aarhus	Geneva	Palermo
Amsterdam	Genoa	Palma
Antwerp	Glasgow	Paris
Athens	Gothenburg	Prague
Bangkok	Granada	Porto
Barcelona	Hamburg	Reykjavik
Belfast	Hanover	Riga
Belgrade	Helsinki	Rome
Berlin	Hong Kong	Rotterdam
Bilbao	Istanbul	Salzburg
Bologna	Kiev	Sarajevo
Bordeaux	Krakow	Seville
Bratislava	Kuala Lumpur	Singapore
Bruges	Leipzig	Sofia
Brussels	Lille	Stockholm
Bucharest	Lisbon	Strasbourg
Budapest	Ljubljana	St Petersburg
Cairo	London	Tallinn
Cape Town	Los Angeles	Tirana
Cardiff	Lyon	Tokyo
Cologne	Madrid	Toulouse
Copenhagen	Marrakech	Turin
Cork	Marseilles	Valencia
Dubai	Milan	Venice
Dublin	Monte Carlo	Verona
Dubrovnik	Moscow	Vienna
Düsseldorf	Munich	Vilnius
Edinburgh	Naples	Warsaw
Florence	New York	Zagreb
Frankfurt	Nice	Zurich
Gdansk	Oslo	

Available from all good bookshops, your local Thomas Cook travel store or browse and buy on-line at www.thomascookpublishing.com

Thomas Cook
Publishing

The publishers would like to thank the following individuals and organisations for supplying their copyright photographs for this book: Aquincum Museum, page 107; City Hotel Pilvax, page 37; Dreamstime.com (Andrey Gatash, page 113; Peter Gustafson, page 33; Udvarházi Irén, pages 122–3; Krzysztof Kordys, page 135; Soundsnaps, page 146; Attila Vörös, page 143); Geopix/Alamy, page 38; Beata Laki, page 71; Pictures Colour Library Ltd, pages 5, 7, 19, 40–1, 59, 75, 85, 99, 102, 118 & 125; Gerrit Prenger, page 64; Claudio Recalcati, page 49; Robert Harding World Imagery, page 131; SXC.hu (Orsolya Ganzler, page 152; Korosy Istvan, page 22; Attila Iván, page 45; Irina Reberšak, page 24); sziget2005.com, page 13; Tourism Office of Budapest, pages 9 & 149; Kádár Viktor, page 141; www.inpixtourism.com (an inpix.co.uk company), page 132; Helena Zukowski, page 117; The Hungarian National Tourist Office, all others.

Send your thoughts to
books@thomascook.com

- Found a great bar, club, shop or must-see sight that we don't feature?
- Like to tip us off about any information that needs a little updating?
- Want to tell us what you love about this handy little guidebook and more importantly how we can make it even handier?

Then here's your chance to tell all! Send us ideas, discoveries and recommendations today and then look out for your valuable input in the next edition of this title.

Email the above address (stating the title) or write to:
CitySpots Project Editor, Thomas Cook Publishing, PO Box 227, Coningsby Road, Peterborough PE3 8SB, UK.